VIENNA

Vienna

VIENNA

*The Image
of
A Culture in Decline*

by

EDWARD CRANKSHAW

NEW YORK

THE MACMILLAN COMPANY

1938

COPYRIGHT

PRINTED IN GREAT BRITAIN
BY R. & R. CLARK, LIMITED, EDINBURGH

TO

A. B. C. AND A. E. C.

WHO LET ME GO THERE

CONTENTS

THE FOREGROUND

LIST OF ILLUSTRATIONS

THE FOREGROUND

I. INTRODUCTORY

THE old culture of Europe is dead, or at its liveliest moribund. Sooner or later another will arise and Western man will persist, no matter how reduced his numbers or frightful his disasters. To reproduce the past, to live it again in the literal sense, is clearly out of all question ; we cannot create or recreate natural circumstances, and on these in the last resort the form of a culture depends. No two cultures have ever been or can ever be identical ; what is dead or dying is eternally unique.

The war of 1914 was destructive enough, but, unfortunately for generalisations, the finest epochs of the many nations do not coincide in time, nor do their checks and declines. Thus, although some picturesque downfalls followed that war, a sort of culture generally survived it ; while on the other hand, for many years, and in some countries more than in others, far-reaching undermining had been effected by the growing industrial spirit, quickening transport, and other deeper causes. This is most true of our own land, which has been dying for a century or so. Even then, the barbaric element has in some curious way preserved some features of the culture it destroyed, as the ice of a crevasse embalms the body of its victim ; but the body is dead. As for the moment, all we can tell is that we are adrift from the cultural tradition which made us, even if everywhere it is not yet wholly out of sight.

It will naturally be asked, What is meant by the old culture of Europe ? But can one really define these things ? There is, of course, an answer ; all of us will have one : my own is this book.

For although civilisations cannot be repeated it may not be idle to contemplate those that are gone : in times of transition, unless one is a popular prophet or a convinced revolutionary, there is little else to do. The air tingles with suspense, structures of great solidity crash to the ground, faint bugles are heard, far away ; something in their accents is portentous, but what does it portend ? Can anybody tell ? And are they north or south or east or west ? Their direction is no more possible to fix than that of a corn-crake in the summer dusk. They mean nothing except that they mean something ; their effect is distracting in the extreme. We hesitate, waiting ; we go on as best we can, now and again, to steady our nerves, glancing back at what we know. We know only what is past. It may not be an attitude of heroism ; instead of standing waiting, waiting until the tones are clearer and their direction plain, it may be more gallant to cast round energetically or let instinct declare a course and follow it headlong. If so, the world is full of heroes at this juncture : a handful less can hardly matter.

Certain things are better evoked than stated ; perhaps they cannot be stated at all. Here, at any rate, I make an attempt to evoke this dead or dying

culture before it lies too far behind. One may read
the past in its monuments, it is said, and here we
have monuments in plenty. Of all these, as I see it
—perhaps with eyes dazzled with love—the most
complete, the most unambiguous, the most comprehensive, the most vivid in its lights and shadows,
the best preserved, is nothing less than a great city
of Central Europe, a whole city—a city which bears
not merely in its buildings but even in its life today
some traces of cultural pride : Vienna, on the River
Danube, capital of the small Republic of Austria,
one time metropolis and administrative centre of
the fantastic Dual Monarchy.

Approximately at latitude 48.15′ North and
longitude 16.20′ East the farthest spur of the alpine
system is broken by the River Danube, towers, in
the Leopoldsberg, eight hundred feet above it, and
breaks off ; on the left bank, save for a weak con-
tinuation of the spur, is nothing but a wide plain
stretching out to the Hungarian Carpathians. For
many many miles the great river has flowed at the
foot of the alpine wall, fed by its snows, and now
at last it leaves confinement and winds out across
the open plain. Rounding the last tall bluff it makes
a sharpish angle with the thrusting spur, and in this
angle formed by the impacting lines of hill and
river, and on the north bank of a little tributary
stream which forms the base of the triangle, some
Celts established a settlement called Vindomina,
protected from the north and west by steep forested
hills, from the south, rather weakly, by the little

stream, from the east by the great river—not, as today, a broad stream flowing swiftly between artificial banks, but a desolate system of channels and swamps which persisted through the ages, providing into the 19th century a lurking-place for scoundrels of every kind. It was, one would have said, a secure enough position in those primitive times ; but it could not defy the Roman military skill, and the settlers were swept away and a fortified camp was established. Vindomina became Vindobona, first a camp, later a Municipium, the beginnings of the modern city of Wien ; to us, Vienna.

To stand on the Leopoldsberg jutting up from the flat river plain, or, better still, on the watch-tower, the Stephaniewarte, which surmounts the Kahlenberg, a neighbouring summit—to stand there and look away to the south is to realise at once the strategic importance of the forgotten Roman encampment placed there to command the Danube and defend the northern marches of an empire. To the left the river, at first a straight and gleaming ribbon, finally curves away to lose itself in the plain of Hungary ; to the right the wooded hills plunge away in countless broken ranges, a tumbled ocean of hilltops closely packed, and above them, very distant but high on the horizon, a pearly cloud hangs constantly, the first snowy peaks of the Alps, the Schneeberg. Between hill and water lies a city.

It is not the city that Beethoven saw from the highest point of his country walks. The villages of a hundred years ago are now built over. Heiligen-

stadt, where the composer is said to have frightened
the cattle by shouting and waving his arms like a
madman, is now remarkable chiefly for a fortress-like
block of workers' dwellings, indicative of Socialism's
craven capitulation to the line of progress marked
out by 19th-century capitalism in its final dropsical
state. Small villas have come to Grinzing and its
vineyards, and from the centre of the city an electric
tram does the journey in less than half an hour.
Vienna, in short, is trying to spill out of her basin.
But even now it is a city within an arena; shouldering out of its midst one sees a shapely buttressed
tower bearing a spire which tapers to a point thirty
feet higher than the cross of St. Paul's : this marks
the moral centre of the ancient city of Metternich
and Mozart, the tower of St. Stephen's Cathedral,
the Stefansdom, "Old Steffl" of the popular songs.
And, although Vienna has expanded lopsidedly away
from the river, which even now it barely touches,
and up into the hills, that tall spire and the far
more ancient tower upholding it still mark the
centre of the city proper, the huddled Inner City,
with walls, bastions and glacis replaced by the
majestic circular boulevard called the Ring.

A ring it is, a shining circlet studded with semi-
precious stones. Not one of its many great buildings
can pass uncriticised, not one is in form and manner
the expression of an inborn tradition ; their architects
worked in the 19th century; yet the cumulative effect
of lightness and grandeur takes the breath away,
leaving little to protest with at the 19th-century
Grecian, Renaissance, and Gothic splendours half

B

hidden by green trees. There is a broad central nave
lined by twin avenues of limes and with more than
a road-breath in carriage-ways and pavements between these and the flanking buildings. It is a
magnificent conception, particularly that great arc
which sweeps round from the Renaissance Opera
House to the Votive Church of the Emperor Franz
Josef with its curious twin spires of fretworked stone.
Between these come parks and gardens, the enormous Gothic Rathaus, the Grecian ("adapted to
modern requirements") Parliamentary buildings,
the Renaissance museums, Burgtheater and University buildings ; finally, standing well back, one
wing set at an angle to the road, that conglomerate
system of buildings rambling over a huge acreage
called the Hofburg, the Imperial Palace of the
Habsburgs. There is no finer street in Europe. It
encircles the constricted heart of a city of two
million people, yet on an April night if the wind is
favourable it is full of the pungent smell of pines
brought down from the mountains fifty miles away ;
on a fine Sunday morning, with no traffic to speak of,
the air quivers with scented waves from the lilacs
in the Rathauspark ; late on a summer evening,
skirting the iron railings of the Hofgarten, once
the Emperor's private ground, you may for a
moment be caught by the remote enchantment of
a Serenade by Mozart played amiably under the
trees and the stars. The sense of the theatrical, of
impermanence, the profoundest of all human
emotions, is accented by the sharp dead greens of
leaves and grass in the white arcs slung across the

road. This is the time when recent past merges with the present; the buildings are the same, the music, the soft night air ; the lights are brighter but no more artificial ; the same single-decker trams with their trailers clatter by like crazy trains ; dim promenading figures break into splashes of whiter light and vanish, leaving the spell intact. This is the atmosphere which helped to give Vienna her legend of romance and gaiety, regardless of the drabness reaching out beyond the magic circle and the tight-packed squalor contained by it. Yet if a city has a flash of true lightness it deserves a legend ; such qualities do not abound. As for drabness, that is unambiguous, the exclusive contribution of the 19th century, of European decadence ; squalor, on the other hand, may bear looking into.

Even now we are far away, though not in space, from what is known as Old Vienna. That lies within the circle, in the shadow of St. Stephen's tower ; and in many spots outside it too, odd clusters of ancient houses and streets, forming all that is left of suburbs in green fields. There are finer buildings in Vienna than any on the Ringstrasse, apart from aspects of the Hofburg—witnesses of the whole course of its culture. But the Ringstrasse, though modern and sometimes garish, is a most striking part of our monument : it belongs to the second half of the 19th century ; it is the last ponderous foundation of a broken culture, built to endure in the service and glorification of a house of kings and emperors which scarcely survived its completion—for fifty years are nothing to a line which has ruled and built for seven centuries. If the city itself is the monument to the flowering of a people, the Ring is the formal admission of its decadence.

The House of Austria

Already in these opening pages, in our first glimpse of Vienna, we find ourselves revolving round the Habsburgs and their palace. This may seem strange : one may contemplate London for a long time before coming to Buckingham Palace : that is not one of the first sights to be seen, unless, perhaps, one is an American. And the development of the ruling house does not spring into consciousness as a symbol of the development of the people. It might be otherwise were the palace more obtrusive. If, say, it were situated on the site long occupied by Messrs. Swan and Edgar, passed by everybody every day, the royal insignia might have become woven into the stuff of our lives. It might. Though the very fact that the position commanding the Hub of the Empire is occupied by a draper, while the royal palace is very much off the map for all of us who do not happen to be season-ticket holders on the western reaches of the Southern Railway, is itself suggestive. The King of England could not live in Piccadilly Circus. Not even if the old houses recently pulled down had made room for a garden for him, instead of ready-to-wear suitings from fifty shillings upwards. And just as surely and inevitably the Hofburg had to be the centre of Vienna, even if in summer its occupants moved to the newer pastures of Schönbrunn.

You get, it seems to me, all the difference in that little contrast. Here, in London, we have a mercantile city spreading out from the banks of the Thames and permitting the Throne to establish itself beyond the gates—and when the gates are torn down it is the City that invades Westminster : the Crown cannot pass Temple Bar without formal permission of the head tradesman, My Lord Mayor. In Vienna, on the other hand, a family with the habit of domination and acquisition occupies a strategic position from which to govern, and a city of soldiers and officials clusters round the family seat, its material needs served by the host of shopkeeping vivandiers which formed Vienna's commerce. The river, the potentially great commercial artery, is neglected, kept well to one side ; instead of being used to make Vienna the wealthiest commercial centre on the Continent (which it might very well have been) it was allowed to provide inspiration for the composers of charming waltzes, who probably never set eyes on the main stream save from a distance—and from the height, say, of the Kahlenberg, it can (in certain lights, and especially looking upstream towards Klosterneuburg) look as blue as can be. For this kind of behaviour the Austrian authorities have earned the gentle reproof of the *Encyclopaedia Britannica* ; but, to set against that, they have provided us with as pretty and clear a picture as exists of the rise and fall of European civilisation, uncomplicated by the mass-production carcinoma which here, for instance, has for the last century or so distracted the eye from deeper, slower symptoms of decay.

Austria, of course, had its own particular complications ; some of them led to the war of 1914. But, on the whole, the culture of decadence has been in Austria stronger than anywhere else and has persisted longer and more fruitfully. Traces remain to this day. Vienna may be doomed, but the Austrian peasant, or some of him, seems to have that quality of imaginative vitality which, possessed also by the Southern French (though in strikingly different form), is able to keep a civilised way of life running like a streak of gold through dark ages.

That, though, is not Vienna. Vienna was Habsburg, today is the Habsburgs' echo—dialectical materialism notwithstanding. Unlike this country, which chose suitable kings from time to time to act as paid figureheads, Vienna was moulded by a family which started ducally to end imperially. The same family for seven hundred years. For seven hundred years the Habsburg line appears to have been intent on only one thing, the accumulation of property, the aggrandisement of its private estates.

The Habsburg Empire did not accumulate in a national search for raw materials or a love of fighting and domination, as is usual with empires. It did not arise from a country's attempt to make itself strong. There was, in fact, no country. There was, in the 12th century, a small province north of the eastern Alps which was made a Duchy by Frederick Barbarossa and changed in name from Ostmark or the East March (Charlemagne's name for the province

created to defend the Bavarian frontier), to Oester-
reich, or Austria. This Duchy was granted to the
Babenbergs, whose line expired ninety years later,
in 1246. After some vicissitudes, featuring Ottakar
of Bohemia, a certain Rudolf Habsburg got hold of
Austria, Carniola, Styria and Carinthia (all, save
Carniola, now provinces of the Austrian Republic)
and divided them among his sons and his ally Count
Meinhard of Tyrol. The first Habsburg to rule in
Vienna arrived in 1282 ; the last, the young
Emperor Karl, departed in 1918. During these
centuries the Habsburgs became one of the greatest
landowning families the world has ever seen. The
first Habsburg property may be regarded as a large
private estate, a feudal estate, that and nothing else ;
and to the last the Habsburgs never saw their
Empire in any other light. For centuries on end
they went on adding further lands to their possessions
with no other motive than pure acquisitiveness and
the desire to defend what they had already acquired.
That is a common enough mania, shared by all of
us, yet here, and perhaps only here, carried to
something like a logical conclusion. This continued
until the amazing family attempted to add Serbia
to the collection. Then they were stopped by the
Allies. On the outbreak of that catastrophic war the
style of the head of the family, Franz Josef, was as
follows : " We, by the Grace of God Emperor of
Austria ; King of Hungary, of Bohemia, Dalmatia,
Croatia, Slavonia, Galicia, Lodomeria and Illyria ;
King of Jerusalem, Archduke of Austria ; Grand-
duke of Tuscany and Cracow ; Duke of Lorraine, of

Salzburg, Styria, Carinthia, Carniola and Bukovina,
Grand-duke of Transylvania, Margrave of Moravia;
Duke of Upper and Lower Silesia, of Modena,
Parma, Piacenza and Guastella, of Ausschwitz and
Sator, of Teschen, Friaul, Ragusa and Zara ; Royal
Count of Habsburg and Tyrol, of Kyburg, Görz and
Gradisca ; Duke of Trient and Brixen ; Margrave
of Upper and Lower Lausitz and in Istria ; Count of
Hohenembs, Feldkirch, Bregenz, Sonnenberg, etc. ;
Lord of Trieste, of Cattaro, and above the country
of Windisch; Grand Voivode of the Voivodina Serbia,
etc., etc.''

Some of these titles were already obsolete in 1914,
but the list gives a sufficient idea of the extent and
scope of the family estates. Other members of the
family, which in 1914 contained archdukes innumerable, had other titles. And for a proper conception of
the Habsburg talent for getting hold of property one
must look beyond the Austrian Empire itself. At one
time Habsburg reigned from Northern Italy to the
Netherlands, and a Habsburg contrived to marry
Spain and the Spanish Empire. In the 16th century
Habsburg all but got hold of us through Mary, our
Queen.

To return to Vienna : even a small estate re-
quires a steward, and this amazing landed property
of the Austrian Habsburgs, with countries instead of
parishes, races instead of local clans, cities instead
of villages, demanded a great army to defend it and
increase it. The central administrative office was
Vienna. Instead of a bailiff with assistants there
was a government with a civil service. Vienna grew

as the estates grew and their populations with them, until, in 1914, it had nearly 2,000,000 inhabitants, most of them directly engaged in administering the Habsburg estates or keeping shop for them. In 1918 the estates were dispersed, to become self-sufficient countries or parts of other lands. But the central office remained, a great city with tens of thousands of officials half starved by years of blockade and with their occupations gone. Vienna began to crumble. There has been no serious check to that process of crumbling until the present day. At this moment this city of 2,000,000 administers itself and a small Republic containing an additional 4,000,000, the majority of whom resent the rule of an effete capital as bitterly as the minorities of the vanished Empire.

It is not entirely accurate to speak of Vienna as the central office. The later Habsburgs were the head of a Dual Monarchy, Emperors of Austria, Kings of Hungary. The Habsburgs have always had trouble with the Magyar, whose notions of the divine supremacy of his own race exceed, at any rate in intensity, that of the pinkest subaltern in the Indian Army in *his*. That is saying a great deal; it is saying as much as one can say. Even then it insufficiently expresses the maniacal intensity of Magyar national pride. These people would be the most charming and delightful in the world—if they had no neighbours. Hungary, then, as an important part of the Habsburg possessions, was intractable. Vienna and Budapest were generally at logger-heads, and during the last phase of the Dual Monarchy Budapest managed more or less inde-

pendently of the Throne the enormous tract of the
Habsburg estates, containing races of every kind,
which came under the head of Hungary. The
stewardship of Budapest was different from that of
Vienna. While the Habsburg family were mainly
interested in land, letting the inhabitants of it, provided they did not think too much, do more or less
as they liked, the Magyars of the Budapest Government were, like the Germans of the Reich, more
concerned with race. The Magyars, of whom there
were, and are, a matter of some four million,
managed their lands, the population of which was
some eighteen million, for the Magyars, this involving a process known as Magyarisation, painful
to non-Magyars and not dissimilar to the Hitlerian
process known as *Gleichschaltung*. It is possible that
an ideal, even an ideal of the kind held and still held
by the Magyars, is more acceptable to the eye of
Eternal Wisdom than no ideals at all. In other words,
that the patriotic fervour of the Magyars, involving
a proud and passionate belief in their own race, is
nobler than the possessive, opportunist temperament
of the Habsburgs. On the other hand there can be
no doubt that the commonplace greed of the Habsburgs caused less temporal misery to others than the
Magyar high idealism. It is a problem. The Magyars
were, and are, patriots. The Habsburgs and their
followers had no country ; they were simply the
Habsburgs and their followers, followers belonging
to every race within the Empire, shorn of national
pride, " Patriots for Me"—Me, of course, being the
Emperor of the day.

It is customary to ridicule the Habsburgs or to abuse them. No high authority has ever escaped the abuse of, at any rate, a portion of its subjects and their champions, the perfectly justified abuse, nor can any high authority escape the ridicule of the philosopher. The Dual Monarchy of Austria-Hungary was, in Mr. Gedye's phrase, a ramshackle affair, but it worked. The Dual Monarchy, particularly the Hungarian half, caused much suffering to minorities. The Dual Monarchy, with its astonishing obstinacy and tenacity where land was concerned, was dull, therefore ridiculous. But it was no duller than this country in its pursuit of raw materials, no crueller in its oppression of minorities than the late minority races are proving to be towards *their* minorities to-day. Even Magyarisation (and the Habsburgs, for all their sins, were never Magyar) has been outdone by Italianisation in South Tyrol. These statements do not constitute a whitewashing of the Dual Monarchy; they are intended merely to remind us that dullness, cruelty and slackness were not banished from the world by the fall of a single crown, however old and heavy. Not even the iron crown of Hungary with the crooked cross. The Habsburgs, it seems to me, were neighbourly enough. Latter-day Austria, like France and England, has never for long let itself be ruled by an abstract idea ; in the days when she did you had things like the Thirty Years' War.

The Austrians, the Viennese, are both very popular just now. In the same breath one hears of their charm and culture and of the awfulness of their departed rulers. The saying that a country

gets the government it deserves is fairly sound.
When the war was over we imagined it disproved
by the enthusiasm with which our emancipated
German cousins sent the Hohenzollerns flying, but
within twenty years they had another Kaiser up,
a super-William, an Adolf, without even the excuse
of a badly managed birth. Kings are always made
in man's image, which is not to say that men never
get the worst of it. A landowner is inevitably blamed
for the evils of his stewardship ; it is only fair that
he should have credit for its virtues. In a paraphernalia like the Dual Monarchy the ruling house, if
it is to be taken into account at all, must receive
acknowledgement as well as condemnation. The
development of Vienna and the flowering of its
decadence was not without its glories. To say that
its rulers did little to encourage them is beside the
point. The remarkable thing is not that Mozart was
buried in a pauper's grave but that he managed to
live at all. This dull, despotic Empire became the
centre of a truly European civilisation. Amongst
other things it bore or encouraged the main stream
of modern music, which some consider the art of
arts ; it had a grand and flourishing theatre; it developed a style of architecture which has made
Vienna one of the loveliest cities in the world ; it
collected together an astonishing wealth of painting ;
above all (and I can think of no more important
achievement in the whole history of our civilisation),
with the assistance of one of its Polish subjects,
Sobieski the Great, it turned back the Turk, saving
Europe for Christianity. In addition to this it became

The Kapuchinerkirche

The Hofburg Gateway and the Michaelerkirche

(and this directly through the Emperor Joseph II) a champion of enlightened medicine, at the same time passionately resisting the dingy tide of industrialisation. Finally, for such as think there may be something in it, it preserved, with many setbacks and lapses and in spite of great intimidation, the truth that life is neither real nor earnest but thinking makes it so. It needs more than a war and a blockade to cause the abandonment of that possession.

. . . . . .

The autumn flowering of Vienna, the iridescence of decay, began with the reign of Maria Theresa, the great Queen who sits hugely commemorated between the twin museums of art and natural history, surrounded by the images of her brave admirals and generals. She stares across the Burgring at the long, cool façade of the Hofburg, with the deep sloping roof and the little squat tower of the Minoritenkirche heaving up beyond. Hers is one of the few sarcophagi in the Imperial vaults of the Kapuchinerkirche to be imperial and elaborate, most of these being plain leaden caskets with that ostentatious lack of ostentation which we consider an essentially English characteristic ; that characteristic which, with us, has its apotheosis in the small gold and enamel plaque in Notre Dame of Paris which records the sacrifice of a million Englishmen that Paris might continue—or whatever.

Maria Theresa encouraged education and provided a daughter to marry the King of France. This charming woman was later to die a fearful death

after making a remark about eating cake if you have
no bread, which was somehow to symbolise all that
the revolutionaries were to rise against. It strikes
me as the first truly Habsburg remark on record,
and the wretched end of the young French Queen
may be seen as the first of those dreadful domestic
calamities which were to befall the house and
culminate in the wretchedest tragedy of all, the
death of the exiled Emperor Karl at Funchal in
Madeira. Undoubtedly Habsburgs had met with
cruel deaths before Marie Antoinette, and undoubtedly crueller remarks had been made by them
than the one suggesting cake as a substitute for
bread. But circumstances alter cases, and in Marie
Antoinette we see for the first time a member of
this monstrous family coming into open combat
with a humanity lined up against her. There were
no more rulers by divine right. France threw over-
board the monarchy ; England's king was on the
throne by invitation of the commoners ; Habsburg
in Vienna now ruled by Our Will in face of a subject
people no longer resigned but ready to show active
hostility ; a changed perspective which hastened the
death of geographical patriotism and strengthened
the ranks of the Patriots for Me.

Maria Theresa, however, saw nothing of revolution ; the royal mother ruled with benign severity
and the daughter still enjoyed the fruits of rank.
She did not call herself empress, but she ruled over
an empire which scarcely questioned her right to
autocracy and gravitated in all its fairest elements
towards the capital city grouped round the symbol

of clerical dominance, St. Stephen's tower, and
hemmed in by great monasteries paid for by the
very populace which the enlightened Queen was so
unwisely and so inevitably playing with the thought
of educating. During her reign Haydn and Mozart
were born.

For all too short or all too long a time after
the death of his mother Joseph II ruled, the
" people's monarch ". An entirely benevolent
despot, a supreme dictator of an enlightenment
we should never dream of associating with dictators today, but even then insufficient. He
broke the power of the Church in Austria, intro-
duced and fostered a spirit of tolerance towards all
things not in opposition to his will, founded the
finest hospitals in the world, patronised the arts
(warning Mozart that his pieces had too many
notes), had one eye ever open for signs of revolution (the first seed of which had been sown by
his mother with her pedagogic zeal, and the tender
plant of which he was all unconsciously shield-
ing from harsh winds), and finally muddled
things badly by trying to emulate Prussia, not
realising—well, quite a number of things, which
we shall have to glance at later. This man was
followed by his brother Leopold, who managed to
straighten out the tangle resulting from the fact
that Joseph was a genius but not quite a big enough
one for his task. After him came Francis, narrow,
pedantic, but amiable, who took the title Emperor
of Austria in 1804, copying Napoleon. He did no
particular good, but managed to hold the forces of

disruption in check. Metternich is first seen in this
reign ; but it is not until the accession of Ferdinand,
a poor wretch, that the Metternich régime got into
its stride. Then Vienna was crowded with spies and
informers and secret police, and the colour of life
grew hectic—until, in 1848, there came the great
revolt and the rulers of Austria for the first time
saw the sort of trouble that lay in store for them.
The avalanche was under way. Nothing could hope
to stem it ; but one man, only half realising the
sort of task he had put his hand to, did his best.
This was the Emperor Franz Josef, who may be
seen as the greatest, staunchest, most unimaginative
stonewaller in history ; even in an age which had
Victoria as Queen of England he stands out. The
flood burst through, of course, taking the Empire
with it, and in the form of a European war. But this
did not happen until destiny had gone to the ex-
tremest lengths to break the spirit of this narrow,
dull, heroic little man, small, square, whiskered, and
speaking with the broadest of Viennese accents. . . .[1]

In 1867 his brother Maximilian, the pathetic,
tragic, betrayed Emperor of Mexico, was shot by
order of Juarez, and Charlotte, his wife, the sister-
in-law of Franz Josef, went out of her mind. In 1889
his heir and only son, the Crown Prince Rudolf,
committed suicide with Marie Vetsera, his mistress,

[1] It may be remarked that, while I refer to earlier Habsburgs by
what may be termed their international or historical names (*i.e.*
Francis, Joseph, Charles, etc.), I have kept to the German spelling
for the last two Emperors, Franz Josef and Karl. This is a purely
personal preference, and quite unjustifiable—except that they were
our contemporaries, and we are accustomed to think of them like
that. Or at least the writer is.

at his hunting-box in the wooded hills at Mayerling near Vienna. In the same year Leopold of Bavaria, cousin to his wife, the Empress Elizabeth, committed suicide. In 1897 the Empress's sister Sophie, Duchess of Alençon, was burned to death in an appalling fire at a Paris charity ball. In the following year the Empress herself was stabbed to death in Geneva by an Italian anarchist. Then, in the summer of 1914, the old man's nephew, Franz Ferdinand, now heir to the throne, was shot at and killed by the Serbian student, Gavrilo Princip—he and Sophie Chotek, his morganatic wife. . . .

That was the beginning of the war, the beginning of the end. It was also the occasion for what was perhaps the last truly Habsburg remark on record. On hearing the news that the poor had no bread, the Queen of France had suggested they made do with cake. On hearing of the assassination which was the beginning of the war, the Emperor of Austria observed, "A higher Power has restored that order which I was unable to maintain . . ." for Franz Ferdinand had been distressingly unorthodox.

" God ", the old man at another time remarked, " has spared me nothing." But there he was wrong. In 1916 he died, thus mercifully escaping the indignity of forced abdication, which two years later fell to the young new Emperor, Karl. In 1918 Karl was an utterly deserted man, his palace at Schönbrunn guarded by two men whom nobody came to relieve. He fled to Switzerland, and, after abortive attempts to return to Hungary, was conveyed in a British destroyer to Funchal, where he died, his

c

weak lungs defeated by the hopeless climate. When he fled Vienna there was revolution, but decadence had gone too far. In 1789 creative vitality had still not died out of Europe. By 1918 it had. That section of the Ringstrasse known as the Franzenring was renamed the Ring of the 12th of November. But the Franz Josef Kai of the Danube Canal and the Franz Josef railway station still kept their names. The bronze eagles on the cornices of the Hofburg still stood silhouetted with spread wings against the evening sky. Only the stucco on the walls of palaces and houses began to crumble.

One does not think of all this when arriving in Vienna. One does not work back into the history of a place until one knows its present. But a brief glimpse must be taken into the past to explain the dilapidated look of ornate façades and the empty desert of the Heldenplatz, the vast parade-ground facing the Burg which has now no Emperor to guard.

II. THE PRATER

WHAT one does think of are a multitude of small and general things which mingle to form an enduring yet elusive impression of the city as a whole : the square granite setts laid down to make the roads and frequently the pavements, and the smooth stucco fronts of houses which have no basements rising straight up from this *pavé* to give the place the air of an 18th-century print with its intermingling of roughness and fine polish; the great breadth of most of the streets outside the Inner City and the lowness of many of the buildings, especially the old-established ones like the Imperial stables on the Museumstrasse which ramble over acres of highly valuable space with the cool disregard of hurry and greed of an Old Regent Street ; the deep and narrow streets of the huddled Inner City, with rows of dormer windows against the sky and tall baroque palaces adorned with every architectural embellishment flanked by disreputable tenements exhaling the odours of mildew and paprika stew, or *gulasch*, through cavernous house-doors ; the extreme and bandbox compactness of the fashionable shopping-streets which thread this area— Kohlmarkt, Graben, Kärntnerstrasse—and are made exotic in effect by the deep contrast of their setting ;

the great open spaces like Am Hof and the Freyung, dwarfing the enclosing buildings ; the innumerable fountains, mostly finely wrought, and always playing —except in winter when they are boarded up against the frosts and become cushioned pyramids of snow; the glimpses through ornate doorways into cool and ancient courtyards ; the " green belt " of the Ring-strasse with its avenues and parks and open places and the great massing of green tree-tops where the Volksgarten flanks the Ring of the 12th of November, hiding whole buildings from sight ; the cheerful and comfortable effect of the expansive plate-glass windows of the coffee-houses, as large as shop windows, but set several feet above the level of the street and yielding glimpses of highly upholstered interiors, heavy chandeliers and people of every shape and size lounging for hours with their backs to the world ; the very peculiar atmosphere pro-duced by the huge, steep-shouldered gothic cathedral in a setting of formal baroque—an overtone of the streets made of granite blocks ; the constantly repeated vistas, at every turning, of high wooded hills shining in the bright, hard air. . . .

And so on.

One gets to know a city first by sitting about in it, then by moving about in it ; then by sitting about for ever. London must be the worst city in the world for the stranger to get acquainted with, since it is the worst in the world for sitting about in ; also, the wild statistics of its chief transport coolies notwith-standing, there can be few places harder (or at any

rate more uncomfortable) to get about in. Paris, I
suppose, is the best place for sitting about in ; but,
taxis apart, its transport leaves a good deal to be
desired. As to cafés, Vienna runs Paris very close,
and, what with its highly efficient but suicidal looking trams, its cheap and abundant taxis, its ration-
alised ground plan (looking from the air like a slightly
wind-blown spider's web with the Ringstrasse for
a hub), it is probably as simple to get about in as
anywhere in the world. Thus, even more than
Paris, it is easy to get to know.

On the boulevards of Paris, and indeed elsewhere, it is customary to sit on a chair at a little
table on the pavement and " watch the world go
by ". This is known as the charm of café life : but
the real charm of café life is something other. It
consists of sitting comfortably in congenial surroundings and talking, or meditating blankly, or reading
the world's press on wicker frames, or looking up
trains in a trans-continental Bradshaw, or having
one's friends drop in on one, or dropping in on one's
friends, or even writing—against the slow buzz of
conversation with the cigarette smoke curling up
into one's eyes and the tin tray on the marble slab
rattling at every movement and the coffee cooling
to lukewarm and then to coffee-cold, the deadest
cold known to mankind. . . . This would be a better
book for being written like that—although now, in
England (it being January), the sun sidling in
through an open window and the sound of thrushes
and early lambs all go to make a cheering substitute.

To return to the charm of café life : if all that

can be done on the pavement, well and good ; in
Vienna, as a rule, it is better done indoors : the
seats are softer and the tables larger. A good
Viennese coffee-house is as comfortable as and no
more talkative than the solidest of London clubs.
There are times, naturally, when one likes to sit
on the pavement, as on a warm summer evening
when the bright lights blaze against the gloaming
with a pleasingly theatrical effect ; but often it is
too cold for this kind of occupation and the habitué
anxious to watch the world go by can always sit
snugly in an upholstered and centrally heated
corner, gazing through the heavy plate glass which
takes the place of the fourth wall. In summer, when
it is hot, these great windows are bodily removed,
and then one sits as in the cool recesses of a deep,
deep loggia, or cave, watching the serious-minded
tourist frying between sun and simmering granite
setts. Within and about one are all the accessories
of a pleasant life, rounded off by many sorts of
coffee, from the finest mocha in the world, through
the Turkish variety in copper vessels (the sole contribution of *that* Orient to the amenities of civilised
life—unless one counts Rahat Lakhoum ?), to the
characteristic, local and opulent *mélange* with its
dollop of whipped cream. With each cup of coffee
will arrive newspapers on frames and two small
glasses of cold water. These will be renewed at
every opportunity, and thus, sipping the waters of
alpine snows (Vienna's water-supply *does* come from
the mountains sixty miles away and is nowhere else
surpassed), one may sit hour after hour for the price

of a single drink, reading, talking, or considering
what to do next—an occupation so pleasant that the
temptation is to do nothing at all—ever.

There is no city in the world where it is more
pleasant to sit considering what to do next, and that,
doubtless, is why, when all is said, its inhabitants
do so little. Anticipation is better than realisation,
we commonly say, but show no signs of taking the
maxim seriously in our sempiternal scramble for
bigger and more lethal motor-cars. The Viennese
don't talk about it, but they have the instinct, though
even they lack courage to make it a philosophy: they
put it down to the *Föhn*, a mild and enervating wind
with an effect on the human tissues similar to that
of the sirocco.

We now, however, must despise the virtues and
delights of *Schlamperei*. We must move about a
little. Vienna is not at its best just now, it never will
be, but it still has a showing to make. Half a loaf,
when it comes to it, has all the advantages over none
at all : you know that if you have ever starved, and
soon cease putting questions of principle. Vienna is
not what it was, but in a few years what will remain ? Perhaps everything ; perhaps nothing at all
to speak of—a heap of ruins, with the knight on
top of the Rathaus suspended head-downwards
from a riddled spire ; and the belief that when he
falls it will be all up with civilisation. Well, so it
will ; but perhaps he won't even have time to hang
downwards a little, before the *Umsturz*. Perhaps, on
the other hand, he will stay up there for ever—as
architecture goes. One cannot tell. But if a continent

is to be destroyed it is a pity to sit about in a café without making an effort to see one of its greatest cities for the last time whole. It is not merely a city. It is, as we have agreed, a monument.

On the other hand this continent still has a chance of escaping annihilation, but only on condition that its peoples try to understand each other, and each other's pasts.

Meanwhile it continues pleasant in our café : the seats are padded and well sprung, the waiters the most amiable in the world, the talking subdued and nowhere strident ; in remote corners young couples, and others not so young, publicly make love with a freedom not encouraged in the north ; on the other hand they laugh and smile more happily than is possible in the north. It is a clear evening in early summer and coolish currents flutter the air. Gentlemen with, to their eternal credit, more leisure than gentlemen of corresponding incomes in this country could ever dream of owning to, play dominoes or mildly flirt or discuss politics, themselves, or the business they have already been discussing earlier in the day in that same place. Others sit reading methodically and omnivorously through an impressive course in international journalism, from the *Pester Lloyd* to the *Illustrated London News*. Women, whose bulk increases in geometrical progression with their age, drink tea of the palest imaginable amber flavoured with lemon, or rum, or milk, or nothing at all, while meditatively devouring cakes of the most cloying appearance and an extreme delicacy of flavour. There is a good deal of talk and laughter, a certain amount of conscientious gloom, an easy hurrying of waiters—who contrive to combine an extreme facility of service with self-respect and an unrivalled capacity for multiplying tips. The place is full of heavy upholstery, shining brass-work, mirrors not tarnished but ever so slightly *faisandé*, extravagant mouldings clinging wherever attachment is possible. There is no music ; just the lazy wave of conversation, the racket of crockery reduced to a minimum. One is reminded in many ways of the reign of Edward VII, which was prosperous for all the world. There are even today in London two or three restaurants where it is still possible to sit in comfort. Of course Vienna also has its modern cafés, and brass too often now gives way to chromium ; but a number of old ones survive—though, alas, fewer than might have done. For during the inflation Vienna committed a cardinal sin : dozens of these established places were pulled down to make room for banks. The people, recovering their morale, soon had enough of banks, but these had done their work. The pressure of the Allied blockade in the immediately post-war phase of the European struggle here reduced a gallant people to starvation. We all know that ; it is to be hoped that we shall not forget it. But what is less commonly known is that the resultant financial anarchy pressed so hard on this last outpost of civilisation that it was driven to deny its own standards, substituting for its coffee-houses, symbols of the cultivated life, the symbols of human wickedness and crassness. We ourselves, in this country, effected a similar substitution so long ago that we have forgotten what it means. It means the beginning of the end of decency. The Viennese did away with their banks as soon as they came to themselves, but the taint remains.

It is still a fine evening and we cannot sit indefinitely indoors, not even in a deep loggia, or cave, with a coolish breeze to flutter the air ; the breeze, moreover, is perceived to be warmed by contact with the hot pavements. . . .

There is no need to go far. We require first of all a glimpse of the people. The inhabitants of a city are that city, and before looking at monuments it is as well to know something of the descendants of the men who built them. Even these monuments, churches, palaces, museums, are interesting mainly as monuments to vanished generations—save the none too common instances where they are also works of art. Even art cannot be wholly separated from the artist.

On a fine summer evening the people of Vienna may be found in many places. In the streets, the little parks, the theatres, the beer-gardens, the cafés themselves. But there is one place above all others which shows a full cross-section of the populace. It has offered that same section, with gradually increasing emphasis towards the left (and, twenty years ago, a sudden atrophy of the extreme right) for the last century and more. This is the astonishing park called the Prater, where rich and poor can both mingle and cultivate their own preserves.

There is no better way imaginable of discovering what Vienna is founded upon than by spending some hours in the Prater ; and the short journey from the Inner City down the Praterstrasse to the Praterstern offers as sharp an evocation of a past that has scarcely ceased to breathe as can anywhere be had.

To some it may mean one thing, to some another : a racecourse laid out on the edge of the Danube plain, a trotting field, a polo ground ; to many more it is a great amusement park of booths and round-abouts and steam-organs in the shadow of a giant wheel rotating with the slowness of a snail ; to some few, perhaps, a strange expanse of wild, magnifi-cently timbered marshland, the last remnants of the old Imperial deer-park, running down to the very banks which contain the swift, dun waters of the monstrous stream. . . . The Prater may mean all these things, and others ; but however many different things it is to however many different people, it is also one thing to them all : the Prater Hauptallee. That is a matchless double avenue of chestnut trees running straight as an arrow, two and a half miles long : the converging lines of tree-tops seem to run together long before the end. The chestnuts were planted four centuries ago—four centuries to a year—when this park was a Habsburg preserve ; and until the deluge came that avenue was the proudest promenade in Europe. Even now in early summer, with the sunlight catching the candle-blossoms, bright against the dark-green

foliage, its grandeur is scarcely diminished. Only—
there are no more parades.

Towards one end, the populated end, there are
three open-air cafés : coffee-houses I, II and III.
These are democratic institutions, backing on the
people's Prater with its cabarets and side-shows. At
the far end, islanded in the broad avenue which
branches to encircle it, stands the faded Lusthaus,
a sort of royal summer-house or hunting-box, now
dim and shuttered. Between the two extremes the
carriage-way lies deserted save for occasional groups
of diminished figures passing from one to the other
of the chestnut aisles, where twilight is deepened by
the pyramidal canopies of sombre leaves.

That main avenue was not designed for walking;
but no motor may pass along it and thus it lies open
still to the muffled ghosts of carriages and pairs.
Barely thirty years ago and they were there in all
their brilliance, and the silence now seems but
thinly to cover the brisk hollowness of hoof-beats,
the creak of burdened leather, the murmuring of
high, smooth-running wheels. And what the ear
discerns the eye will reinforce : the parade is
on. . . .

No longer summer twilight but the brilliance of
an afternoon in May with all those chestnuts in full
blossom ; no longer a desert ribbon but a stream of
leisured carriages—horsed with the pride of ancient
stables, driven by cockaded coachmen, hoods down
—the glistening transport of an amazing regiment
of women with cavaliers as outriders. They revive
themselves with the sunwashed air after long wilting

hours in the hothouses of fashion. They are the
cream of Vienna's world, and half-world too. The
wives and mistresses of statesmen ; singers, actresses,
fashionable cocottes ; princesses from all the lands
of the Empire, from northern Poland to the hot
coast-lines of the Adriatic, proud and passionate
Hungarians, proud and aristocratic Bohemians of
the most ancient families—the greatest Patriots for
Me ; and mingled with them the native Viennese,
dowagers and chaperoned young girls, fair, sentimental, disarmingly cynical, and with an aura of
innate gaiety. . . . All these run the gauntlet of a
historic promenade. Slowly they drive down the
interminable vista and, circling the Lusthaus, drive
slowly back, the horses chafing at the turn. And all
the way in the brilliant transparency of the Central
European air ; all the way exposed to the judgement
of their peers—with a smile at an instant's command,
a gloved hand ready to wave.

The illusion fades. The jingle of the flashing
brass dies away ; the last hoof-beats echo hollowly.
They came and are gone and the great park is left
to the people ; the people of Vienna, compact of
innumerable races, Slavonic, Latin, Teutonic, people
from mountain valleys, forests, moors and fertile
plains, now all Viennese—stamped with the unique
badge by mingled circumstances, the enervating
Föhn, the proximity of the East, the sense of in-
habiting the Kaiserstadt of an enormous empire.

Now the parade has gone for ever, but the people
remain and they are not much changed.

It is never easy to draw the line between the

distorting generalisation and the illuminating one, but generalising about national characteristics is a time-honoured amusement and has the support of the most august authorities. About the Austrians, for instance, one should not generalise ; one would have to ask first, who are the Austrians? A tiresome question to answer. But the Viennese are quite another matter : they are simply the people who live in Vienna, and their city is compact and homogeneous enough and strong enough in character to put its stamp on everybody native to it. Vienna to the Viennese is a very different matter from Austria to the Austrians : in the one you have two million men, women, and children crowded into a few square miles, sheltered by the same hills, subjected to the same climatic idiosyncrasies, grouped tightly round a core of common tradition ; in the other there are people of the plains and people of the mountains, men and women living on the verge of other countries and influenced by them—Germany, Switzerland, Italy, Jugo-Slavia ; whole pockets, like the department of Carinthia, cut off by mountain systems from free traffic with their neighbours ; the Catholic Church as the sole unifying element. The Viennese, however, are—the Viennese ; from the highest to the lowest, and all in much the same way. And in that way the inhabitants of Greater London are no longer Londoners.

That is an 18th-century spirit—or what we mean here by the 18th century ; something that we have lost. For Vienna is a centralised city, which London, four times too large, is not. The cultural centre of

all Vienna is bounded by the Ringstrasse, while
London has no such centre—the Hub of the Empire
consisting now of a cinema, a draper's shop, an
insurance office and a statue ; instead, the inhabitants of Golder's Green and Streatham are
beginning independent centres of their own. The
result, one feels, will be unsatisfactory, with less
tradition behind it than the Middle West of America.

Vienna is not as big as that and never can be now.
The older city was packed closely enough round its
churches, its palaces, its theatres, its ruling family,
its red-light quarter and its ghetto ; and although
it has expanded greatly the ways from the remotest
parts are still open to the centre. There is no ruling
family now, no ghetto or red-light quarter as such ;
but the other amenities of civilisation remain, and
you may still walk down the Graben or the Kärntnerstrasse knowing for certain that you will have to
raise your hat every ten yards or so—a formidable
undertaking in that city where the rules for greeting
acquaintances are as strict as the orders pertaining
to " paying compliments " in the British Army.
Five yards of each ten, then, are walked demon-
stratively bare-headed. . . . Or, if you do not shop
in Bond Street, the same will apply to the Mariahilfestrasse, the interminable bourgeois shopping street
running from the old Imperial stables almost to
Schönbrunn. That can be said of neither Bond Street
nor Tottenham Court Road.

In fact, no country can be called uncivilised so
long as its metropolis retains certain attributes of a
decent market-town ; and, conversely, civilisation

vanishes the moment the individual can feel lost in any warren. You can't have a social conscience when the individual feels that he is unobserved. The complex, of course, is not as simple as all that, but a certain passage from a novel by the wretched Marquis de Sade seems capable of expansion : " One has no idea how sensuality, and indeed anything else, grows with the knowledge of safety ; as soon as one can say to oneself, ' Here am I, alone, to all intents and purposes at the end of the world, far removed from prying eyes, where no creature can come near me ', all obstacles and restraints are swept away. . . ." De Sade there speaks specifically of lust- ful pleasures, and in 18th-century Paris he could find that perfect immunity only by locking himself up in an empty house. But in a community so large and decentralised that the individual is overlooked there must, quite plainly, be a slackened sense of responsibility. Vienna, in so far as she has preserved her atmosphere of a country town, for all her two million of inhabitants, and in so far as it is still possible for all ranks to indulge in gossip and scandal about all ranks, remains to some extent a centre of civilisation. One day a book will be written to show the prophylactic functions of gossip—which, like other remedies, can also kill.

Vices and inertias of some kinds are never checked, however—community ones, which persist simply because every one is so firmly in their grip that nobody troubles even to pretend that he is not. And without this pretence there can be no gossip. The municipal vice of Vienna is a sort of laziness, an

easy-going spirit which quickly degenerates into slackness. The quality is recognised by the Viennese, who
are not hypocrites, and called by them *Schlamperei*.
It is shared by the highest and the lowest, causing
the former to lose battles, the latter to forget errands
—both for insufficient cause. This is not the virtuoso
carelessness of the Southern French, the languid
procrastination of the Spanish, nor the militant
unreliability of the Italian. It is something quite
charming, frequently annoying, ultimately disastrous, and for ever catching its victims unawares.

Nor was the ruling house immune from the
weakness of its children. One finds what is probably
the first considerable act of Habsburg *Schlamperei*
occurring in the summer of 1315, when the two
brothers, Frederick and Leopold of Habsburg, lost
the chance of an offensive against Louis of Bavaria
in order to get married, although nothing less than
the Crown of the Holy Roman Empire was at stake.
And, dropping down the centuries, the war of 1914
would at least have been postponed (with the chance,
when it came, of having it unambiguously nailed to
Prussia) had it not been for *Schlamperei*. For instance,
it should have been known, and doubtless in some
responsible quarters it was known (though not in
the chambers of the Hofburg), that the unfortunate Archduke Francis Ferdinand would never
come back alive if he went to Sarajevo. He was sent
there, just the same. Princip was not the only figure
in those crowded streets keyed up to a homicidal
exaltation. And if he had missed, another might not
have done.

That should have been known in Vienna, and in certain hidden places doubtless was.

And of course there was plenty of *Schlamperei*, pitted against the crudest evil, in the negotiations before the final declaration of that war.

We begin, however, to get a wrong perspective. Touching lightly on a minor vice of the Viennese, which is also the source (or the corollary) of so much charm and poise, we find it pointing the way to treachery and carnage. But in its everyday appearances that vice is transformed into an amiable weakness, unfateful in visage, unspectacular in effect. And even in its farthest-reaching mood its action is by no means always cruel. The old bureaucracy, with Franz Josef at its head, which governed the late Habsburg Empire was described by Viktor Adler as "Absolutism modified by *Schlamperei* "; and without that modifying spirit, very analogous to the spirit of muddling through which has so strengthened our own country in its possessions, the Dual Monarchy would have foundered long before it did. It is not too far-fetched to say that it only foundered in the end because one half, the Magyar half, shared the Prussian incapacity to learn how to take things easily. Taking things easily is the mark of the civilised spirit and at the same time the unmistakable stamp of decadence. So what is one to do ?

That, I suppose, is the riddle of the Sphinx ; and one may be pardoned for doubting whether even she can know the answer.

Not that there seems to be much choice in such

matters. You cannot arrest the decay of autumn
leaves at the moment of utmost gorgeousness, nor,
distrusting mellow fruitfulness, can you spend your
life in a state of vernal greenness. The leaves must
wither, fall and rot, leaving bare branches until
another spring ; and although the affairs of man
move slowly and a long, long winter is an age of
darkness, winter also has her glories.

It is easy, people may say, to achieve light-
heartedness and elegance when you have no worries
—meaning, of course, that the favoured inhabitants
of a Kaiserstadt with a vast empire of oppressed
provinces to batten on live remote from the great
realities of life. But in the years before 1914 only
a fraction of the Viennese lived thus remote, a
similar fraction to that found in any metropolis ;
the bourgeois emphatically did not, and the poor
were dreadfully poor. And even today, with nothing
to lean on but herself, Vienna still has about her
that aura of gaiety, in spite of the crumbling stucco
and the empty pockets and the vanished future ; it
is more than a matter of bright uniforms and dash-
ing horsemanship—though these were superbly
appropriate in that setting. Vienna is still a light-
hearted city. Her armies were annihilated in the
war, her civilian population almost starved to death,
and now, for eighteen years, she has stood like an
overcrowded fortress, cut off from the world, beleaguered by hostile forces at all points of the compass
and betrayed within her gates. In Western and
Central Europe only the peasant of the devastated

areas can speak with equal authority on the realities of life. And, as for the past, we shall see before our tour is ended that no place has dwelt more constantly in the shadow of the elemental forces. Vienna has seen the worst, has had those fingers at her throat, has been crippled by them. Yet she is still gay.

I use the word gaiety to describe the peculiar quality of the Viennese because it is the one in common currency. But the Viennese are also human and they have their sorrows which weigh as heavily in that lovely city as beneath the smoke and murk of northern manufactories. Or almost as heavily. As keenly, certainly ; even more keenly, perhaps ; for there is no diffusion, no confusion of a general depression of mind with the sharp pang of the particular sadness, such as we find up here. The gaiety of Vienna is, indeed, a peculiar mixture of fact and myth. Nowhere is found more resignation and nowhere less self-pity. The legend of careless abandon started, no doubt, in the time of Metternich, who staged the frivolities of the Vienna Congress to keep his diplomatic visitors amused and mellow while he adjusted the map of Europe to his liking. But it must also have been sufficiently characteristic in the last days of the Empire, and even now it is by no means dead, bursting out at odd times and, during the weeks of carnival, with intoxicating freshness.

But although the Viennese are supremely capable of frothy enjoyment on occasion, their everyday mood, which also has a refreshing lightness, is something other. It is closely bound up with a sense of futility and impotence, which, free of self-pity, finds

expression not in hysteria or petulance but in a sort
of cheerful cynicism masking an inner blankness.
Some of the causes of this, and some of the results,
we shall understand before we leave the city : it
pleases or exasperates according to one's mood.
Behind it is some weakness but also a good deal of
unmelodramatic courage.

This is not so far as it may seem from the Prater
Hauptallee with its flaunting chestnuts, its ghost
of a procession ; for in that great park you will find
even today traces of the vital contrast between the
sorrowful and the gay, the crude and the highly
polished, which belongs, in this country, to the 18th
century ; something that we have lost but which
for the Viennese is not utterly extinct, though long
past its apogee. You will find that atmosphere in-
corporate in the very street which leads from the
Prater to the fashionable quarters of the Ring. The
Praterstrasse more than any other thoroughfare is
a perfect relic of more spacious days, and yet twenty
years ago it was alive, a most imposing carriage-way,
carrying from the palaces and mansions clustering
round the southern arc of the Ring the whole of
Viennese society, from the Hofburg downwards,
for its ritual tour of the chestnut avenue. It is
wide enough to take in a broad area of sky and the
flanking houses are tall enough to collect the light and
reflect it with all the luminousness of a Canaletto.
Many of the house fronts are stuccoed—that stucco
now peeling off in strips—some are adorned with
graceful mouldings ; and the roadway between

those ornate fronts is of blocks of hewn granite. It was here that Johann Strauss the younger lived and composed his waltz of the Blue Danube, taking to himself Schubert's discoveries about the use of wood-wind and brass together and so assimilating these that the tones which were once peculiar to a great Viennese composer too serious for the understanding of his fellow townsmen became for ever the unmistakable badge of that city's emotional colour.

And if the Praterstrasse is Johann Strauss it is also the setting of the triumphs of another Viennese of the Viennese: at No. 31 stands a dilapidated-looking theatre, still used, but quite devoid of character; and it was here that the astonishing Johann Nestroy, actor-manager-playwright, satirised Vienna in the time of Biedermeier. He is forgotten now. One of his fantasies with a fantastic name, *Lumpacivaga-bundus*, is still occasionally played as a curiosity ; but in his day he was a power, and there is still a freshness in his works. It is not to the credit of Vienna that he is forgotten. He lived in the middle of the 19th century, but he had the 18th-century eye, seeing life as Hogarth saw it; and in him more than in any other, as in this street more than in any other, we see a prolongation of that age of apotheosis. Even, I feel, until 1914 the spirit of that highly organised procession of society which passed unheedingly before the empty shell of Nestroy's genius was closer to the dead century than to its own. Vienna had no 19th century as we understand it, or even as the Parisians understand it. The 18th

slowly waned and then with that calamitous up-
heaval the 20th was suddenly, starkly there. But
though circumstances can suffer violent change you
cannot uproot a people in a night, though with
the rising sun they will twist their heads to face
the source of warmth. And passing up this desolated 18th-century street (built, as building goes,
largely in the 19th century) one arrives at that
unique enclosure, the Prater, where even today one
may look at life as Hogarth saw it, as Nestroy saw
it, as Strauss felt it, as the promenading aristocracy
from the Schwarzenburg quarter, remote yet rub-
bing shoulders with a cheerful populace, may have
vaguely sensed it. . . . The inevitable contrast between silks and rags, but both with feet on a rudely
metalled earth, the broad sky above : which is so
infinitely different from the contrast between the
mass-produced limousine and the mass-produced
factory wage-slave.

The poor of Vienna are neither mass-produced
nor elegant, but they have great reserves of cheer-
fulness which is best displayed in precisely the
booths and cafés of the People's Prater, in the cafés
and *Lokals* of their native districts, in, on occasion,
the beer- and wine-gardens on the lower slopes of
the Wienerwald. They can be very poor indeed,
making ends meet, somehow, on an income that
would barely pay the rent of an English labourer's
cottage. Eating and drinking forms one of their
acutest pleasures and to it they bring much understanding, yet fresh meat is a luxury and six days out
of seven they live on next to nothing. They live,

thousands of them, in conditions of, by English standards, squalor. Yet squalor will, as we have said, bear some looking into, which drabness, not even of the most respectable kind, certainly won't. And indeed this squalor in the last analysis is usually found to be a matter of ventilation—or lack of it. You get that stuffy smell of unaired bedrooms ; its, to English nostrils, suffocating atmosphere of frowstiness. And on top of that the ceaseless smell of paprika stew, or *gulasch*. And on top of that the cloying reek of cheap Egyptian cigarettes. Often these people live in picturesque courts, alleys, lanes, with low-ceilinged rooms, mouldering, shut off from air. But if one realises that air in the house is not sought, the picture clears a little. Boarding in an unfashionable district with the penniless widow of a small official, the writer was given notice for insisting on having his bedroom window open in mid-winter. The proper procedure, in October, was to seal the double windows, confining a scarlet sandbag between the two panes to keep out the draughts ; that arrangement not to be tampered with until spring. And of course one slept covered by that curious form of feather-bed. The writer, by opening his window, was putting not merely the other inhabitants of that flat but also the whole immense apartment building with 113 stairs in danger of pneumonia. He had to go. . . . So that stuffiness which is responsible for much of our horror in face of continental slums, if it is not minded by the lower black-coated class will hardly be minded by the labourers and porters. And the picture, it seems

A Courtyard in Mariahilf

The Burgtheater on the Ringstrasse

to me, is lightened still further if we remember that
certainly Schubert, and almost as certainly Beethoven and Mozart, lived in just that atmosphere of
unaired bed-clothes, *gulasch*, narrow courts, and
windows hermetically sealed. This may have affected
their health ; it probably did : but it did nothing
to subdue their spirits. Could a Schubert, one
wonders, flourish in the drab, hygienic *parages* of
Tooting—or even in the super-barracks of municipal
flats proudly erected by the Socialists and later
shelled by Major Fey ?

Not that Vienna is lacking in drabness. Drabness,
in fact, as with all great cities, is the first impression
on arrival at the termini. Whether or not Vienna
was ever fully 19th century in spirit, she lived
through that monstrous age, whose monuments
sprawl grimily over what were once vineyards and
fields in the shape of rows and rows of tenements
surrounding the factories of Ottakring, Hernals and
elsewhere. Such drabness is insufferable. It was in
revolt against this that the Socialists raised their
Marxian barracks, not against the easy-going squalor
of the older portions of the city and its suburbs. But
even here the drabness cannot kill. At almost any
point the Viennese, oppressed by bricks and mortar,
with the sense of the earth underneath soured by
decades of immurement, can lift up their eyes to the
hills shining so very near in summer or in winter
standing aloof and virginally white. Even the earth,
one feels, is not altogether dead. It has so many
breathing holes, so many small and decorative parks
where the soil is still fresh, not poisoned, as in the

more northern cities, by the corrosive acids created and broadcast by man in his search for the millennium. The Viennese on the whole are sceptical about the millennium. They would call it a year, like any other. They are inclined to make the most of what they have instead of burning it up in the blind hope that from the ashes glory will arise. That kept a check even on the activities of the 19th century.

I say the Viennese ; but the fact that Vienna is not London or Detroit is tremendously due to two men ; the Emperor who ruled throughout that baneful period and the burgomaster, Anton Lueger, whom for so long that Emperor fought. For Vienna is, or was, in a position to become the greatest commercial and industrial centre in all Europe—having the Adriatic ports so near her gates, the coal-fields of Bohemia close at hand, and the great arterial Danube to control. Yet apart from some inevitable smears that grisly era passed her by. The dynasty protected her from the rule of tradesmen and the magnificent burgomaster saved the small man from the trust and combines of meglomaniac lunatics. . . .

It may be, however, that this is not the kind of thought that passes through the heads of the people in the Prater ; the Viennese are not noted for reflection, this having been discouraged by the same rulers who discouraged the financial jamborees of Aryans and Jews. That place, the Prater, is now in full swing. The twilight has deepened and from the shadows of the lonely avenues and paths gaiety is manifest in coloured lights glinting through the

trees and the distant strains of a waltz. One realises
how unanimously the heart of this great city beats
to a lilting rhythm which supports tunes now gay,
now melancholy, " *qui caressent le cœur sans y péné-
trant* ". It is the rhythm of everyday, from the café
concerts of the Prater to the hand accordions of drab
streets. Even now it resists the invasion of American
jazz, which is widely played and admired ; and even
in sophisticated haunts there will sometimes be two
bands : one to play fox-trots with a solemn, self-
righteous air and a most unyielding tempo, one to
start up the waltz, the signal of relaxation. It is
made to carry a thousand moods. Sometimes the
familiar cadences will seem to reflect the purest
carelessness of heart, a naïve mingling of gaiety and
nostalgia ; sometimes it revolves with mechanical
weariness, an ancient, bedizened body with a
tenacious spirit ; sometimes there is a droning
quality, as though that rhythm were the mainspring
of some dreadful motor actuating all the puppets
in the world ; sometimes it is a deliberate and calculated self-intoxication ; but again it may be a veritable
uprush of spontaneous laughter, playing with senti-
ment for fun ; sometimes the chequered progress of
a dream.

In the Prater after sunset it has a peculiar
quality. The air is cool and it grows dark ; the last
gilding has been rubbed from the summits of distant
hills ; close at hand, but out of sight, the great
Danube flows quietly by towards the advancing
night. All life is dead in the outer darkness and the
attention and hope of the universe seems centred

on this flood-lit patch of gravel beneath mighty trees festooned with coloured lights. Somewhere a band is playing—a waltz, of course—its resonance lost beneath the space of the stars. Within that magic circle small tables are set out on the gravel, spread with checked cloths, at them people eating, drinking, gesturing, unreal in the glare of the floods, hedged in by black shadows picked out with scarred tree-trunks and stagily green leaves. As we approach we catch the faint clatter of crockery ; figures grow more distinct, and as we break into that charmed circle the atmosphere suddenly changes from that of a mystery to that of a burghers' Saturday night. . . .

Suddenly, but by no means stridently : these are the Viennese of, on the whole, the lower middle classes, and though on their drinking nights there is a certain heartiness and readiness to appreciate horseplay there is much less readiness to practise horseplay, and the laughter and voices, though perhaps raised, are diminished by the open air. The dialect is, moreover, soft, broad, very pleasant to the ear, in the mouths of the cultured an amiable drawl, but not unlike broad Yorkshire in the more emphatic intonation of the labourers. . . . This crowd, then, quiet enough, intent on its beer, its garlic-flavoured meats, generous, but paying due attention to the destiny of every groschen, is, even close to, distinctive enough. Vienna is not ironed out to the international level ; she is the greatest provincial city in the world, having all of the good and much of the bad of provincial cities everywhere, and, on top of that, the standards of a metropolis. . . .

By provincial I mean that Vienna lacks that quality
of taking herself for granted as the only place in the
world that matters ; this distinguishes her from
London, New York or even Paris. To the Viennese
Vienna *is* the only city in the world, far more
emphatically than London is to the Londoner; but
he is very conscious of it. His pride is no different
in kind from the pride of the Liverpudlian—only,
it happens to be justified. All the assets of his city
must be shown off in public, though deprecated
scurrilously in private ; whereas the citizen of your
polyglot metropolis, your metropolitan man, your
Londoner, your New Yorker, will deprecate his
assets publicly with a show of fervour, still knowing
in his heart that they are unsurpassable. The provincial lacks that bland, unthinking arrogance. He
has to boast a little.

You notice this in the dialect, of course. That was
spoken—possibly as a matter of policy, possibly not—
by the Emperor himself, and the finest old gentlemen
were content to talk that easy-going, drawled idiom
which takes the rough edges off the German language. The loathing of the average Reichs German
for the Viennese accent amounts almost to disgust.
Whether this is due to an inferiority or a superiority
complex it is difficult to say unless one is oneself a
German ; and then one wouldn't bother to ask why.
Inferiority, probably ; there is something very
feminine about the Prussian, something masculine
about the Viennese ; the Prussian, like the Suffra-
gette, has no reserve : his cards are continually being
slammed down on the table, even the ones most

palpably marked. His manner of speech is to match.
The farther south you go the nearer you get to the
Viennese drawl. You can't drawl, naturally, without
a good deal of inner assurance. But the Viennese like
to show that they know the best High German when
they hear it, and so the Burg Theatre has become a
sort of shrine where the tongue may be venerated
as a light which burns eternally. That, too, may
irritate the Prussians.

You notice it also in the clothes. Vienna is perhaps the only Western capital which preserves what
amounts to a national dress. That, of course, is not
the leather shorts affair of the alpine provinces,
though you run into these a good deal worn both
by the genuine provincials with business in the
abhorred wen and by young men from the suburbs
about to scale the heights of the Kalhenberg, half
the way by tram. The national urban dress is a
different affair ; half our middle-aged friends in the
Prater are wearing it on this magic evening. It
consists of a stiff little hat in darkish green with a
ribbon of brighter green, a narrow brim and a
shaving-brush of chamois hair up behind—to prove
that one has never shot a chamois. Or it may be
the lyre-shaped tail-feathers of a blackcock. That
may be worn with or without shorts, but it goes, as
a rule, with a coat called a *Jopve*, a sort of shooting-
jacket generally of a coarse fabric in rather dull
checks with leather patches where the sleeves have
been worn through. But it is in winter that the
characteristic figure is most plain. Your true
Viennese, rich or poor, wears no full-length over-

coat. Instead he has a short coat reaching half-way down his thighs and topped with a heavy fur collar. That gives you the characteristic silhouette ; the figure bulking large at the shoulders, supported by long, thin legs, the *Gemsbart* sticking up jauntily from behind the little hat. To complete the silhouette you stick into the mouth one of those long thin Virginian cigars with a straw running through. The result is unmistakably Viennese.

And although the women have no national dress they too are unmistakable. Apart from the Parisians the Viennese dressmakers are the only ones capable of creating style, and the Viennese women know how to maintain it. And so genuinely creative is her dressmaker that no Viennese dressed in the height of fashion could be mistaken for a Parisian, and vice versa. Whereas the fashion-plates of every other land are interchangeable.

You notice it also in the food. England has roast beef, eggs and bacon, and many other excellences ; but every *Wiener Schnitzel* made is a homage to Vienna, and the local method of cooking everything is pursued to the very fringe of the international settlement of the Kärntnerring. There is no compromise—even over *Rindfleisch* where, heaven knows, some compromise is needed to temper the dullness. (But *Rindfleisch*, dismally boiled lumps of dismal beef, is not confined to Vienna ; it seems to indicate a flaw in the whole Central European complex.)

All this municipal patriotism is more important than it may seem. Vienna is frequently called the city without a soul ; but indeed it has one, a little tattered, weary, on the surface very unexacting, but, in the last resort, tenacious. This legend of soullessness is based on second impressions, and the second impression is the bane of human intercourse, being, in one way or another, responsible for nine-tenths of human misery. All quarrels of whatsoever description are based on the uncontrolled sway of the second impression, on the fear of being taken in.

The first impression is mindless, warm, intuitive. Our magic circle beneath the trees is a first impression. And so is our vision of a carefree people sitting out their lives in cafés over coffee or *Gespritzes*. So is the conception of Vienna as a place where everyone can sing. In all that there is some human truth. But the second impression, which sooner or later comes to us all and where sooner or later most of us stick, is a thing to avoid altogether or else to keep watch over until we have had time to reconcile it with the first. The first impression is mindless, the second no less. Fresh from the lilacs of the Stadtpark you run into one of those dreadful cripples of the war, legless, an aluminium plate where the back of his head should be, his eyes protected by dark goggles, who in Vienna are, or were, turned loose by the Municipality to beg in the streets seated on little trolleys which they propel along the pavements with two bricks held in mittened hands for oars : or you land yourself in some small trouble with the authorities and find yourself up against *Schlamperei* in real earnest : or you find beneath some smiling, courteous, solicitous exterior an eye for the main chance which would confound a non-conformist urban district councillor in the provinces of England. And you react accordingly : behind all that good-humoured elegance is corruption and decay ; and we all know, of course, that a white-washed sepulchre is a thousand times more noisome than one which no one has troubled to prink : it is apt to take us in, and that is a sin against the Holy Ghost. In other words, the second impression, when the first has been good, is almost inevitably a bitter reproach for what at first sight was hidden from our sight. It is called " seeing through things ", the supposed key to all wisdom—as though the substitution of one fixed and limited focus for another had some special merit. . . . The third impression consists of reconciling the two opposed points of view, both of which have some validity. For though our fury with a people for hiding their skeletons from the first casual glance has no conceivable relevance, the skeletons nevertheless exist.

Vienna, at first sight the most glamorous of cities, suffers badly in this way ; for the more abandoned the first delight the more bitter the subsequent fury. What was charming and light-minded becomes bedizened and bottomlessly cynical; what was a passionate love of the arts becomes the cover for empty-mindedness ; what was courteous is insolent hypocrisy.

Vienna, in short, is a smiling face without a soul. Give me, any day, Plain Jane ! The Viennese, while gravely apologising for an admitted deficiency, will

E

raise a sceptical eyebrow in the direction of Plain Jane—and proceed to make herself up.

Perhaps things are different now. The plain English visitor will still get indignant when he discovers that his charming Viennese are entirely deficient in a sense of values—*his* values. The plainer American will fret at the absence of moral uplift. But the serious critic, he who is really serious and was once hurt that the Viennese were not, is less sure of his ground. The Viennese admitted decadence sooner than we did; the Habsburg rule made it easy for them; but we are all decadent together now; the millennium is not at hand; we too are abandoning the quest; and all the apparatus of that search—the increasing paraphernalia of civilisation—is rusting on our hands for lack of directive confidence and will.

We suffer the tragedy of Plain Jane, whose dullness has got her nowhere in particular, regretting the lost days when we too could have had our fling instead of keeping the basement dusted for an inspection that was never to be.

It is all very difficult indeed. . . .

THE BACKGROUND

III. THE STEFANSDOM

THE time has come to glance at a deeper past, a past now manifest in scattered monuments of stone. Not that these will take us a great way back; there is nothing much in Vienna dating back beyond the 13th century, and very little as old as that. There are Roman remains, of course : Vindobona was a border fortress, important enough to be visited by Marcus Aurelius, who died there ; but Roman remains are much the same the whole world over ; they belong, moreover, to the history of European civilisation as a whole, not to the story of its most recent culture. That was built up on those foundations.

Nor need we bother a great deal about the days of Charlemagne, who is always made too much of in Vienna. There is nothing whatever dating from his time unless one burrows underground. That is to say, for example, that what is now the baroque church of St. Peter's, standing rather splendidly in its little Platz just off the Graben, was once another kind of church, founded by Charlemagne, it is said, in the 8th century. But since there is nothing of Charlemagne about it now that hardly seems to matter ; the ancient, early Christian house of worship has become a brilliant baroque edifice with an oval-shaped dome of green copper. That process is fairly typical of Vienna.

As for Charlemagne and the Habsburgs it is customary to speak of the Emperor Franz Josef (or, to be accurate in inaccuracy, the unfortunate Karl) as the last of Charlemagne's successors. That is very romantic, but it ignores two facts : the first, that the Holy Roman Empire was formally dissolved by the act of Franz Josef's grandfather, Francis I ; the second, that although most of the Habsburg rulers from the middle of the 13th century were also German, or Holy Roman, emperors, practically all the virtue had departed from that office long before the Habsburgs first partook of it—five centuries after Charlemagne's death. Thus, the only noticeable connection between Charlemagne and the Habsburgs is the legendary sword in the secular treasure chamber of the Hofburg, a handful of other more authentic relics, and an antiquated title. To make much of this connection would be, it seems, to strain a little.

For the purposes of sightseeing the founder of modern Vienna was Ottokar of Bohemia, who in 1278 was defeated by Rudolf of Habsburg ; but for the purposes of enlightenment we may glance a little further back still.

We ought to do this because it helps us to understand the strategic importance of Vienna as a bulwark against the East, to realise, for instance, that Metternich's famous phrase, " Asia begins on the Landstrasse " (that being the main thoroughfare of the eastern district of Vienna now called after it), is a great deal truer than most epigrams, in spite of Budapest ; also the story of Vienna in the early Habsburg days is so undistinguished by attention to the humanities that, without a realisation of its peculiar position, it would seem a parvenu among the European capitals.

Vienna as a settlement or a town has, we already know, more or less always existed, but it would be a mistake to think that when Charlemagne founded his Ostmark he found there a miniature city all ready for him. On the contrary, Ostmark had no particular value in itself ; it was regarded as an eastern bulwark for Bavaria, in rather the same way as France is regarded by contemporary British premiers. Bavaria was what mattered, not Ostmark. Ostmark was a sort of no-man's-land, full of Charlemagne's wire ; and after his death it was overrun, and large parts of Bavaria too, by Slavs and Magyars. The true history of Austria hardly begins for another two centuries, when Otto the Great, the Holy Roman Emperor of the time, achieved one of the first decisive battles of modern Europe on the Lechfeld in the summer of 995, thereby freeing Bavaria of the Magyars and paving the way for the nominees of his son to do the same for Ostmark, or Austria. But the Lechfeld is a long way from Vienna, and when his son, Otto II, conferred the East Mark on a certain Leopold of Babenberg in 976 its capital was at Pochlarn on the Danube, some half-way between Vienna and Linz ; but the process was started, and, by gradual stages, the frontier was pushed down the river, and with it the seat of government, or capital, until, in the middle of the 12th century, Vienna was reached, via Melk and Tulln. The Magyars were pushed well back.

It may be asked why the defeat and rolling up of the Hungarians was so important to Europe, one way or the other. Why should it have mattered that Teutons instead of Magyars colonised the northern borders of Italy ? Possibly it didn't matter much, but one is inclined in the light of subsequent events to think that it may have mattered a good deal. The subsequent events were that as recently as the 17th century the Magyar territory of Hungary was colonised by the Turks, who, with the connivance of the Magyars, repeatedly used that area as a jumping-off ground for assaults on Austria. So that if the Magyars had retained their run of Austria, Asia would probably have begun not on the Landstrasse but somewhere in the middle of what is now, thanks to Vienna, perfectly European Europe. And what would have happened to Italy ? Venice performed miracles, but she could not have defended the alpine frontier.

However, the main thing is that the Babenbergs, nominees of the Emperor Otto II, secured Vienna. Shortly after that Ostmark was raised from a Mark to a Duchy and finally rechristened Oesterreich, which is its name today ; and when, a hundred years later, the Babenberg line expired, Austria was more or less what Austria proper was until St. Germain —in spite of the best efforts of the last of the Babenbergs, called Frederick the Quarrelsome, to ruin the work of his predecessors. Of these the greatest

had been Leopold II, who was a patron of the arts
and a protector of the Minnesingers. He was called
the Glorious. Beneath his rule Vienna, already the
capital, achieved a position as a mediaeval cultural
centre analogous to that of its final flowering in the
18th century. It bore for a time the standard of
civilisation, and although that state did not last
for long its position as a city of first importance
was established. Walther von der Vogelweide sang
where shortly before wild nomad tribes had pitched
their tents. Vienna was—Vienna.

Nothing remains to be seen of that city. Its
heyday was the end of the 12th century and the
beginning of the 13th. There is no church as old as
that, though possibly the romanesque remains
attached to the utterly dull little church of St. Rup-
precht on the Franz Josef Kai of the Danube Canal
may be allowed to count. Those who are curious,
however (and it does throw some light on the
appearance of that ancient city with its mediaeval
court), may care to be reminded that when Vienna
became the capital of the Babenbergs the city was
so small that the southernmost fortifications ran
not on the Ring but on the Graben, now to all
intents and purposes the centre of the Inner City.
The original church on the site of the cathedral was
actually outside the eastern city walls, which ran
down what are now the Rotgasse and the Kramer-
gasse. The northern wall was lapped by the waters
of the Danube's southernmost arm, which has now
been tamed to form the stagnant Danube Canal ;
while the western limits are marked by the Tiefer

Graben, which joins with the Naglergasse, the extension of the Graben itself. The shape of the streets as seen on the map shows quite plainly the shape of that very ancient city; and the great square called Am Hof, just inside the junction of the western and southern walls, was the site of the Babenberg castle. Even today one can recapture the atmosphere of a fortified place in that tangle of streets and narrow lanes on sharply different levels which extend between Am Hof and that other great square, the Hohermarkt, which was once the Roman Praetorium. This insignificant square, no more than a quarter of a mile from side to side, lost now in the circle of the Inner City, was the germ of modern Vienna. Most of our business will be outside it, but it should not be forgotten, for, although there are few monuments, and none at all as old as we could wish, this in all Vienna is the only space of ground that has the authentic smell of infinite age.

The bonds were burst by the Babenbergs themselves. So rapidly did the place expand beneath their beneficent rule that just before their extinction this energetic family was forced to erect a far wider circle of fortifications. These were built, it is said, by the ransom money paid for Richard Lionheart, held a prisoner in the castle at Dürnstein higher on the Danube. These new walls did not come down until the end of the 17th century; they were needed to defy the Turk. Until the middle of the 19th century an open glacis lay between the ancient bastions and the outer districts. Then the Ring was built.

Idle curiosity may take you back to the wooded hill called the Leopoldsberg, the Danube cliff whence we had our first view of this city, and where, until the 16th century, there stood a castle which had been the seat of the Babenbergs until the final move down into Vienna and Am Hof. The name of the man who made that move, the last stage of a toilsome and adventurous penetration on the part of the West into the East, following always the wooded, cliff-life banks of the Nibelungen stream, Heinrich Jasomirgott, is commemorated by a modern monument and by a little street running west from the Stefansdom into the tangle of lanes in the heart of the Inner City. That is all. From now on, save for one long and one brief diversion, Vienna is Habsburg.

The first diversion occurred before ever the Habsburgs arrived. It was provided by the election of King Ottokar of Bohemia as their ruler by the people of Austria and the neighbouring provinces, who were weary of the troubles arising from the feebleness of the Babenbergs' successors. Ottokar came in 1252 and left just twenty-six years later, having restored some order and built a great church to St. Stephen on the site of the old one which once stood without the walls. Ottokar was the most powerful prince of the German, or Holy Roman, Empire, and logically his line should be the rulers of Vienna to the present day. Instead, that rule was transferred, when barely established, to a family very much inferior in power and standing, a family called Habsburg, who then began to show the first signs of that lust for land which was for centuries to remain their principal characteristic. They were by no means a local family; they came from the upper reaches of the Rhine. There is about their removal to the Danube some quality which reminds one of latter-day colonisers overseas who leave their limited possessions in an established order to seize and hold great tracts of virgin land, cheerfully dispensing with the charms of civilised society for the compensation of knowing no restraints.

.   .   .   .   .   .

From the tower of St. Stephen's, from the dead centre of Vienna, there is a view of a most imposing kind. The city itself is seen whole : in the clear air its limits are perfectly discernible ; it appears as a great town, which it is, resting on the bosom of the natural earth—not as an endless, dingy plain of bricks and mortar. The eye is first caught by the skirting hills with their beech-woods green, fresh, and very close, the bluff on the extreme right being the Leopoldsberg, the early seat of the Babenbergs, " the Cradle of Austria ". But if one turns one's back on those hills one finds oneself looking away past the river at a flat, dullish tract of land which has been of more importance to Vienna than all the Wienerwald ; not to Vienna alone, but to Europe as well. That low-lying, moist tract of ground, enclosed by the Danube and its small tributary the March, is a traditional field of battle. It is called the Marchfeld.

One is looking, then, across the venerable city in its shining setting at one of the great arenas of

Europe; perhaps *the* arena; and one is standing on
a platform high above the tenements and palaces,
a platform on a tower which, for centuries past,
has been a landmark for advancing and investing
armies; a tower, plainly visible across the plain,
which has been the focus of covetousness of many
races, Slavs, Prussians, French, Hungarians and
Turks—a landmark for invaders, and the standard
of Habsburg might.

The undistinguished-seeming plain had blood
on it long before the House of Austria was founded,
long before Vienna was even a small town. It must
have been the scene of innumerable forays from
prehistoric times to the beginning of our era. We
hear of it first when the Romans fought the Marco-
manni in the time of Marcus Aurelius, and men
continued clashing there in constantly increasing
hordes until at Wagram, in the high summer of
1809, the French and the Austrians between them
lost nearly sixty thousand from a total of three
hundred thousand men. But Wagram, though impressive, was less a decisive victory than a sign of
the times, of the imminent downfall of the Habsburg Empire which stood, in all its imperfection,
for the culture which we know, which may be called
the second Christian era, which now is rattling in
its throat. With the defeat of Napoleon six years
later and, most suitably for this book, the Congress
of Vienna, the avalanche had started which was to
smash up all we know : the results of that accident
we call the age of progress ; certainly things have
moved.

More interesting to us are those great conflicts in which Habsburg held its own in defence of the Western world and Christendom ; and from this point of view the most spectacular occasions had to do with the repulsing of the Turk, against whom Austria has for ever been the bulwark. But in spite of this the very first important battle there, though less obvious and striking, was also perhaps the most important of them all, holding as it did the seeds of all that followed. It was perhaps the most important of European battles anywhere. It is called, suitably but vaguely, the battle of the Marchfeld, and it was there that Rudolf drove out Ottokar, securing for Habsburg the Central European focus.

Until the advent of this Rudolf the Habsburgs had been landowning gentry in a smallish way with their headquarters in the neighbourhood of Strasburg. Rudolf himself was no more than a count, but in middle age he was elected Emperor of Germany, or Holy Roman Emperor, in recognition of various convenient qualities : he was extraordinarily liberal for those days, having a marked sense of *noblesse oblige* ; he was extremely able ; he was a tactician of genius—it is said that he was the first man since Alexander to hit on the expedient of a bridge of boats ; at any rate, he crossed both the Rhine and the Danube in that way ; he was also capable at any moment of devising stratagems as simple and effective as the wooden horse of Troy ; finally, and most importantly, he was insufficiently powerful to be a nuisance to his tributary princes.

For the Holy Roman Empire of Charlemagne's dream was even by the 13th century more of a conception than a fact. It was not quite a shadow, however ; some of the electors which it leagued together still regarded the Emperor as their supreme temporal head, while most of the others obeyed him when they felt inclined to ; and each new election was a solemn business. Rudolf, as we have said, was elected partly on account of his excellent parts, partly because he was conveniently weak. Ottokar of Bohemia, the nearest thing to a true Imperator then existing, was far too powerful to make an acceptable choice, and from the very beginning this Ottokar proved a thorn in the flesh of Rudolf, refusing to pay his dues. Finally, when late in life Rudolf developed personal ambitions and, deciding to increase his hereditary family dominions (which stood quite apart from his elected office), chose for that purpose the provinces of Austria, Tyrol, Carinthia and Carniola, the trouble grew serious indeed, for just those provinces were held by Ottokar. The rest was the battle of the Marchfeld. Ottokar was killed. Vienna, with Ottokar's new cathedral, became the Habsburg family property—not all at once, for Rudolf had taken the lands from Ottokar in his capacity as German Emperor, and it needed some little time before, still in his capacity as German Emperor, he could transfer them to himself in his capacity as a private landowner. He managed it, however ; he was not a Habsburg for nothing ; and this employment of an Imperial might, which was not hereditary, to defeat a private indigence, which was, is somehow typical of Habsburg politics for ever after.

That was the true beginning of the House of Austria. In the year 1282 this tenacious and not ungifted family, represented by a soldier of genius who was also astonishingly liberal, moved from the Rhine to the Danube and settled there for the next seven hundred years. The Habsburg dynasty, as distinct from the Habsburg accident of Roman Imperialism, was founded. It was founded on that marshy tract now overlooked by the tower of St. Stephen's, and its history is the history of our culture.

As for our point of vantage, the south tower of St. Stephen's, that was not yet built. But the church itself owes its origin and some of its present shape to Ottokar. In his day it was all in a style of late romanesque, and today there are relics of that edifice substantial enough to justify our starting from that point and older by far than anything else in Vienna except a few stones here and there—and, of course, the Roman remains. The Ottokar part of the cathedral is, apart from the gothic south tower, also the most imposing. It forms the basis of the whole of the west front, which is chiefly notable for the great door called the *Riesen Tor*, or Giant Door, and the two curious flanking towers called the *Heidentürmen*, or Heathen Towers. And although today we are standing in the great tower with the spire, the two Heathen Towers of the ancient building must have been perfectly visible from the field of battle. Probably they were the last things King

Ottokar saw of the new city of his pride; they have
stood very well.

Most ancient churches have been freely built
about on, but in many the disunity of style is
sufficiently disguised from the superficial glance.
With the Stefansdom, however, the more superficial the glance the more monstrous that building
seems. It is only to the loving and sympathetic eye
that this great church, at least from the outside,
is a beautiful thing. By then one has abandoned
architectural for humane standards.

Never in any building can succeeding generations
of architects so blandly have ignored the message
of their predecessors. However passionately the
exponent of gothic may believe in the pointed arch
as the true and unique gateway to salvation, however contemptuously the draughtsman of the
renaissance may feel towards the incoherent barbarities of an unseemly past, however complacently
the 19th-century restorer may rest assured that in
his hands lies all the wisdom of past ages to be
distributed by him in nicely balanced dollops—one
expects, one would expect, all these gentlemen to
take at least some care with the joins, if only for the
ultimate glorification of their own separate panaceas.
Not a bit of it, not at any rate in Vienna. The
cathedral of that city is crammed with fine bits, by
any standards beautiful ; the whole, to the unsenti-
mental eye, is a colossal lesson in art history. Gothic
is added to romanesque, baroque to gothic, 19th-
century enlightenment to them all, with the air of

F

a man dumping sacks of potatoes. Each section has
the unremittingly rigid air of two neighbours at a
party denying acquaintance. The charming romanesque west front with its two round towers and its
lovely door turns an unrelenting back on the sweeping gothic nave ; the abortive north tower is
astonishingly snubbed by a renaissance cupola perfect both in form and irrelevance ; the great south
tower, achieving its aspiration in a tall, slender spire,
stands over the transept with an air of more than
semi-detachment from the 19th-century roof, like
some Italian campanile, only purest gothic. That
roof, a monument to 19th-century junketing, is
beautifully symbolic—a smooth, steep slope of highly
glazed tiles of many bright colours done in a herring-
bone pattern of extreme clarity which is interrupted
by a colossal emblem of the double-headed eagle
sprawling all over the choir. At first, one seems to
remember, one gasps at this apotheosis of lavatory
tiling, but later the shock is absorbed, and before
long the Stefansdom without its astonishing roof
would be no church at all ; certainly not the
cathedral of Vienna.

One doesn't look at St. Stephen's as at an architectural essay, but sentimentally, as at a friend and
protector. Its blunt and cheerful omission to pretend that it is anything but what it is, is seen to
comply to an unwritten and probably unconscious
Viennese rule of conduct. Nobody, not even Franz
Josef, ever tried for one moment to pretend that
there was anything particularly unified about the
Habsburg Empire. The various lands were so many

private properties and on state occasions the Emperor addressed his subjects as " My Peoples ". He was quite content with that, provided they were his ; there was no need to pretend that the Czechs, the Slovaks, the Serbs, Croats, Slovenes, Magyars, Poles, German Austrians and Bessarabians were all Austrian to the core. Provided each was loyal to the landlord, the tenants could think what they liked of each other, nor was there any obligation for them to model their customs on those of Vienna. That showed a singular, an almost naïve, lack of hypocrisy : one possessed so much land and one added other bits as one might, just as architect after architect added bits to St. Stephen's. There was no point in pretending it was all of a piece. It wasn't. Why worry ? It was all done in the service of the Lord.

And if that patchiness of the premier house of worship is typical of some quality essentially Viennese, the general appearance of the church also has a correspondence with the people of a kind far less abstruse. You see it standing there on a sultry summer's day with an air, unique among churches, of having been dumped there at a handy spot, of standing benevolently at ease. That, possibly, is also due to its curious shape : having no unity of design, its form expresses no idea. There is aspiration in the southern tower with its air of turning its back on the rest, but it is an aspiration severely frustrated and held earthbound by its stunted neighbour capped by its candle-snuffer in renaissance work. The romanesque west front puts up a show of grandeur, reserved and a little aloof: but the pose

is completely ruined by the background. The gothic
arches flanking the nave soar heavenwards only to be
borne down by the roof of shining tiles. . . .

It stands there comfortably up from the pavement, the tall spire smiting the blue, the tiled roof
glittering hotly under an almost southern sun. Inside, one knows, it is cool, and for a great church
unusually dark (there are no clerestory windows),
an enormous vaulted space with a groined roof
upheld by eighteen stone pillars as thick as ancient
limes, the gloom broken by brilliant bursts of colour
from side-chapels in baroque; and, far off, at the
end of that dark avenue of columned stone, the high
altar blazing silently, like a jewel with an inner
light. . . .

The Stefansdom is that—the dim, cool interior
with its sombre Rood looming through mists of
incense, its illuminated shrines, its smouldering
chromaticism of stained glass—that and the conglomerate pile dumped down in the square where
the three chief thoroughfares of the Inner City
meet—the Rothenturmstrasse, leading down to the
canal, the Kärntnerstrasse, to the brilliant Ring,
the Graben, reminding us by its name that the
ancient city of Vienna was bounded not by the
bastions of the Ring but by a lesser circle, so small
that the oldest church of St. Stephen stood just
outside the walls; there is also the Schulerstrasse,
where Mozart lived.

It is an emblem. On our somnolent summer's day
it is peacefully at one with the slowly moving atoms
at its feet, with the long row of sleeping taxis

dumped down in the middle of the Graben beside the curious open-air café also dumped down in the middle of the street, like a child's play-pen, furnished with tables and chairs and a few giant striped umbrellas. On a day of this kind the unaspiring pile makes no demands upon the spirit, and the Viennese, I think, are grateful.

Whether the tourist will see this I don't know; perhaps if he stays long enough, moving slowly enough, he will. If not, there is plenty in Baedeker to compensate him, a good deal of the 14th century. The most perfect single part, perhaps, is the astonishing pulpit against the third pillar on the left as you walk up the nave towards the choir. This is highly decadent 16th-century gothic, a sort of final fabulous flowering, attributed to Anton Pilgram of Brunn, in which the sandstone is made to serve the purpose served by ivory in the miraculous carvings of the East. The most interesting single part, probably, is another pulpit installed behind iron bars in a recess on the outer wall of the apse on the Schulerstrasse side. From this pulpit in 1481, though not on this spot, St. Capristanus is said to have agitated against the Turks.

But St. Stephen's, though Baedeker can make it interesting enough, is in some ways more a manifestation of the people of Vienna than of the history of kings and statesmen. Partly, perhaps, because coronations did not take place there but in the Augustinerkirche; partly, perhaps, because kings and princes do not rest there (with one or two exceptions) but in the Kapuchinerkirche. And even today, after a term of Socialist rule in a city long famed for its ungodliness, it is bound up with the lives of the people. You go there to satisfy a mood rather than a curiosity; to listen to the magnificent organ flooding the sanctuary with sound ; to hear High Mass with music composed by men who were very much of the people : Schubert ; Bruckner. . . . Nor has it to be summer for one to realise the humanity of that place. In winter when an easterly wind comes streaming over the plain from Asiatic wastes you will see in the lee of the west and southern walls all the pedlars of Vienna with naphtha-lighted stalls full of Christmas toys and bright red images of Crampus. That great roof, transfigured by thick snow, shows with a pale effulgence against the night sky, while the steeple, darker, stands on guard.

.   .   .   .

It was not long before the parvenu Habsburgs started improving the cathedral they had won from Ottokar, but the story of Vienna during the century that followed, though full of incident, is unenthralling unless one is going into it with a thoroughness uncalled for in this book. It is the story of a slow emergence from the chiaroscuro of the Middle Ages into the Renaissance. Save for one brief and chaotic interlude the Habsburgs held Vienna, and Vienna was the capital of the senior member of the family ; but its development as a cultural centre was hampered to a formidable degree by two things : first by its situation as a border fortress commanding the

Hungarian plain; secondly by the absence in the Habsburg economy of a law of primogeniture. Both these considerations make of the early Habsburg history a tangle of conflicting interests which all but defies unravelling. There were so many of them, functioning independently and frequently in opposed directions, and things are complicated beyond measure by struggles within struggles within struggles. The Church had its own policy, the Emperor had his (it was not until later that the Imperial Crown came to be regarded almost as a lawful Habsburg perquisite), the various Electors had theirs, the various Habsburg provinces had theirs. This muddle persists from the end of the 13th to the end of the 15th centuries; indeed, from the moment when Rudolf I divided his newly acquired lands among his sons until the moment when Maximilian, the last of the Mediaeval Habsburgs, collected them, if only temporarily, beneath one sceptre. He was only just in time, for things had reached an unholy climax, with the King of Hungary in Vienna and the Turks all over the eastern provinces of Carniola and Carinthia. But he was in time, and it was he who refounded the quaking house.

It is understood, I suppose, that although these early Habsburgs were sometimes emperors they were never kings. After Rudolf the Holy Empire grew more hollow every day, and at the close of the 15th century this tremendous alliance of the Christian lands that might have been seems in many ways to have resembled the latter-day League, that

also might have been, of Nations. One gathers a
vivid impression from an address of the volatile
Aeneas Sylvius, who, before he became Pope Pius II,
was in the service of the Emperor Frederick (Habsburg) III. The address is to the Germans :

" Although you acknowledge the Emperor for
your king and master, he possesses but a precarious
sovereignty; he has no power; you obey him only
when you choose; and you are seldom inclined to
obey. You are all desirous to be free ; neither the
princes nor the states render him what is due; he
has no revenues, no treasure. Hence you are involved in endless contests and wars; hence also
rapine, murder, conflagrations, and a thousand
evils which arise from divided authority."

And so on. Substitute "League" for "Emperor"
and we feel very much at home.

We see that the Imperial Crown was less imposing
than it might have been, and if we consider the
meagreness of the lands which the Habsburgs could
actually call their own we shall not be surprised to
find Vienna remaining so long an inconsiderable
city. Austria, when Rudolf defeated Ottokar, was
a duchy, that same duchy founded by Otto and
handed over to the Babenbergs. With it Rudolf took
over a number of other duchies, or counties : Styria,
Carinthia, Carniola and Tyrol. These, except for
Carniola, which is now in Jugo-Slavia, form the
present Republic of Austria, which, as we know, is
a very small country. But in the early days of the
Habsburgs there was no such unity. All these parts
belonged to the Habsburgs (for Tyrol, given to his

ally Count Meinhard by the first Rudolf for services rendered, was recovered by a later Rudolf), but, because of that stultifying absence of any law of primogeniture, they were ruled by various brothers. It was not until Maximilian that they all came under one hand. They never in all their history formed a kingdom. If we recall our list of Franz Josef's titles we shall see that he was, amongst other things, Duke of Salzburg, Styria, Carinthia and Carniola, Archduke of Austria, and Royal Count of Tyrol. Vienna, thus, was no more than the capital of a duchy, later an archduchy, ruled over by the senior brother of succeeding generations. The other brothers had their own cities, Klagenfurt, Graz or Linz, and Vienna was merely the greatest among these. What is more, these provinces were frequently at loggerheads; they rarely combined to help each other. While the ruler of one was sowing seeds in his garden outside the city walls the ruler of another would be smashing his head against the brick wall of the Swiss, whose toughness the Habsburgs took a very long time to realise.

Vienna, of course, was growing all the time ; but not notably as a cultural centre. The Habsburgs were too busy pursuing the arts of death to have much attention left for those of life. Things might have moved more quickly if, instead of frittering away their energies in futile individualistic wars of conquest in the West, they had all combined to stem the menace of the East; but that incessant task devolved upon the ruler of the easternmost province, whose capital was Vienna.

It was not until the middle of the 14th century that our city had its first real breathing space. The new ruler was Rudolf IV, called the Founder, who had the sense to realise that Switzerland was not for him and give his attention to lands nearer home. It is in his reign that we see the first gleams of the Renaissance, soon to light all Italy. He made Vienna a centre of some brilliance, pomp and culture, and he founded a university which was the second in all Germany, and started to enlarge the Stefansdom. He died young, but we see in him signs that he vaguely realised the holy Habsburg mission, and to him belongs the credit of first thinking that Austria should be an archduchy; to this end, indeed, he forged a remarkable series of documents, proclaiming himself an archduke and claiming all manner of privileges for Austria on the strength of them. The Emperor of that time, however, not a Habsburg, wisely put a stop to that; but he could not know what stuff this family was made of.

Rudolf was succeeded by an Albert of a placid and philosophic nature, but little strength. He seems to have started the Habsburg custom, culminating in the iron bedstead of Franz Josef, of living in extreme simplicity at the core of splendour. He also was stirred by the filtering light from Italy, spending most of his time between the abstract sciences and gardening, while his fiery brother, Leopold, lost improbable battles against the Swiss. And then, after his death, came a period of hopeless and appalling chaos, with brothers quarrelling like cats and dogs.

Internal peace did not recur until the accession of
a fifteen-year-old boy, another Albert, later to become another Habsburg Emperor and a man with
qualities of greatness. Besides making Austria a
quiet island in a dissension-riven Germany, this
Albert (Albert II as Emperor: Albert VI as Habsburg) managed to do brilliantly by his possessions
as a reward for supporting the Emperor Sigismund
against the followers of Huss. He was the only
tributary prince to dare the blast of the Reformation
by supporting the then Emperor and representative
of Rome, and for that service he ultimately received
the kingships of Bohemia and Hungary as well as,
on Sigismund's death, the Imperial Crown. In him
we see displayed for the very first time that Habsburg championship of the Church of Rome which
for centuries was to be its sustaining policy, amongst
other things leading to the Counter-Reformation
and the obscenities of the Thirty Years' War and,
as we shall later see, the weakening of the morale
of our city itself.

But all that has yet to come. For the moment the
process of Habsburg aggrandisement seems to have
made a glorious start, but suddenly, Albert dying of
dysentery aggravated by a surfeit of melons con-
sumed in a river-campaign against the Turk, chaos
returns. Habsburg loses Bohemia, loses Hungary,
retains only the shadow Crown. In the person of
the Emperor Frederick, who looks like being the
last of the family to have anything to do with our
city, it also loses Austria (with Vienna), Styria and
Carinthia.

It was this Frederick who was served by Aeneas Sylvius at the time when he apostrophised the Germans. Nor was Sylvius exaggerating. Frederick had so little power of his own that on his journey to Rome for coronation at the hands of the Pope, through country of which he was the supreme temporal head, he and his insignificant retinue would have been at the mercy of any casual mob. He was sublimely weak. Succeeding to disputed lands (for Albert left a posthumous son called Ladislaus, round whom the most fantastic complications raged), he entirely lacked the ability, or even the will, to bring order out of chaos. There were qualities in him which have persisted in various Habsburgs right down to Franz Josef. He was full of the most exalted ambitions for his house, and incapable of doing anything to realise them. While losing extensive territories, while seeing Vienna itself in the hands of Matthias Corvinus, the Hungarian King, he found time to invent the famous motto " A.E.I.O.U.", which he had carved, engraved, or stamped on everything he owned. That, he triumphantly disclosed in his will, having (with some discretion) made a mystery of it all his life, meant " *Austriae Est Imperare Orbi Universo*", or, in honest German, " *Alles Erdreich Ist Œsterreich Unterthan*". That is very much the kind of thing Franz Josef might have said, with his empire breaking up beneath him. Another favourite saying was, "It's no use crying over spilt milk ", or, more exactly, " To forget what cannot be recovered is the supreme felicity ". And that is almost precisely what Franz

Josef said after Solferino, on which battlefield he lost the treasured provinces of Italy. He might have been, in fact a Franz Josef of a pre-bureaucratic age.

Not that he had no triumphs. It was Frederick who succeeded where Rudolf had failed and at last raised Austria to an archduchy; it was Frederick who rather startlingly evoked from his loins the man who was to be the second and final founder of the Habsburg greatness, Maximilian I; and it was Frederick who laid the first stone of that foundation by marrying this Maximilian to Maria of Burgundy, this being the significant forerunner of that unending series of brilliant political marriages to which the Habsburgs owed so much.

The Renaissance, the European rebirth, has, after a long delay, begun to spread from Italy across the barrier of the Alps, to Austria and Vienna.

But although the Renaissance has reached our city its influence for many years will be restricted. Nothing is gained by comparing Vienna with Paris or London in their early development. Indeed, we should feel surprise not at Vienna's backwardness but at the fact that in her exposed position she managed to become a cultural centre at all. For, at the risk of repetition, it must be realised that the rôle played by the Viennese throughout the slow rise of our culture was the inhabitants of a border fortress. One does not expect to find a highly developed culture on the North-West Frontier. Quetta watches that Delhi may hold Durbars. And through-

out the first five hundred years of Habsburg rule
Vienna lived behind thick walls that in Paris and
London men might dream. A small wonder then,
that when the tension broke, the Viennese, relaxing,
should have gone the pace and run through the
stages of civilisation, arriving at the decadent stage
in advance of her soberer, more disillusioned sisters.
Whatever one may say against the Habsburgs, their
duties as Marchers should never be forgotten. What
Europe owes to them is quite inestimable. The fact
that they brought ill as well as good is neither here
nor there, nor that they were not moved by altruistic
motives, but played for their own hand all the time;
their own hand on so many occasions happened to
coincide with the European hand, and the Habsburgs
being nearest to the trouble had to cope with it
alone. Whatever may be said in theory, if any family
deserves to have after its name the letters FID.,
DEF., that family is Habsburg. " To this family
does Europe owe its preservation." The worthy
Archdeacon Coxe could write that sentence in 1817.
Later in the 19th century the truth was obscured
by the belief that European civilisation had hardly
begun. It is time it was visible again, this time surrounded by a nostalgic aura unknown to the old
historian, who himself must have mistaken (and
how inevitably) the first brilliance of decay, lighting
up his times, for another step towards the peak as
yet unattained. "To this family does Europe owe
its preservation. In this house has Providence placed
the barrier which arrested the progress of the
Mahometan hordes, and prevented the banner of

the crescent from floating over the Christian world. United with the Catholic Church by interest no less than by passion and prejudice, its chiefs were, for a short time, the great opposers of truth, and the oppressors of civil and religious liberty. But adversity taught more tolerant and liberal principles ; and, as Austria first saved Europe from Mahometan barbarism, she has since formed the great bulwark of public freedom, and the great counterpoise to France, in political balance. At all times, and in all circumstances, Austria has been pre-eminent in peace as in arms ; the court of Vienna has invariably been the great centre on which the vast machine of European policy has revolved."

When Coxe was writing those lines, the very cadences of which reflect the decline from the 18th century, the wheel, unknown to him, was coming full circle ; " the great oppressors of civil and religious liberty " were already reborn in Vienna. And beyond it another power was rising, Prussia, a power to which no counterpoise existed, or could ever exist ; for Prussia, in the years that followed, far from showing any appreciation of the rules of the game, displayed a blind and total incapacity to realise that there was a game at all.

" To this family does Europe owe its preservation " : and as that family declined Europe declined, dying with it. In the 11th century the Babenbergs cleared out the Magyars and settled in Austria. At the end of the 13th century the first Habsburg to move from the Rhine started the final consolidation of the frontiers. With the widening of the nave

of St. Stephen's the new culture of Europe was
rising fast. With the adding of the roof it was over.

.   .   .   .   .   .

All that remains, then, of pre-Habsburg Vienna,
is the romanesque part of St. Stephen's—unless one
counts the very early 13th-century relics in the
Rupprechtskirche, a church so uninteresting and so
foolishly restored that it is not worth visiting. With
the rest of St. Stephen's, and with the trinity of
ancient churches which always, to my mind, symbolise the beginning of modern Vienna, we are in
Habsburg Austria, and there we stay. The three
churches are the Augustinerkirche, the Michaelerkirche, and the Minoritenkirche. They are all in
the Inner City, but in the south-western area between the Ring and the site of the ancient fortifications, and clustering round the Hofburg. The Hofburg was started by Ottokar in the lee of the new
walls where the Ring now runs, the ancient area
round the Hohermarkt and Am Hof thus being
finally abandoned by the ruling house, for the Burg
has been inhabited by Habsburgs since the time of
Albert, son of Rudolf, who died in the first decade
of the 14th century. Our three churches all belong
to the early years of the Habsburg sway, two of
them, in their main structures, providing a tangible
link with the very beginning of the Habsburg
dynasty which we cannot find in the Hofburg itself,
for the oldest surviving portion of that belongs to
the middle of the 15th century—the chapel, or
Burgkapelle, headquarters of the celebrated boys'

choir to which Schubert once belonged.

Of these churches one, the Augustinerkirche, has a closer association with the Habsburgs than the fact of its existence throughout the whole of Habsburg time. It was known as the Court Parish Church ; in it the later Habsburgs were crowned ; while in the Chapel of St. George beyond the altar are a series of urns containing the dust of Habsburg hearts. It has been extensively remodelled and restored, but, from the outside, it still retains an appearance of great age, standing wedged in against the Augustiner bastion almost adjoining the Hofburg itself, its slender tower with the 19th-century top-knot dominating the deep and narrow Augustiner-strasse. The Michaelerkirche, on the Michaelerplatz opposite the Rotunda of the Hofburg, has no such associations, but somehow, with its charming gothic tower, capped by a copper spire of nice proportions, the whole surmounting a façade done in 18th-century classicism, it is a reflection of Viennese lightness and inconsequence, a little slice of Austrian history culminating in the 18th-century flowering. The Minoritenkirche is made of sterner stuff. That, to the present writer, is the most precious silhouette of the whole city, a curious, asymmetrical, ugly duckling of a church, a great sombre hunchback of a church. Standing isolated, very properly, in the Minoritenplatz, which leads from the Ballhausplatz with its fateful Chancellory, itself in the shadow of the Amalienhof of the Burg, it somehow contrives to dominate Vienna with a strange and alien sturdi-ness. It stands there as though shaking a burden

from its huge steep shoulders, which reach up,
irregularly, almost to overshadow the tall, untapered,
square-topped octagonal tower, sparsely loop-holed,
stiff, aloof, like the stem-piece of a Northman's
galley. It is somehow lovable in its patient immo-
bility ; it is also a shadow of stern reality. It has
outlasted a good deal of brilliance and froth. It will,
one feels, if left to itself, outlast a good deal more.
It is a touch of Austria in the heart of Vienna. It is
called the Church of St. Mary in the Snow. . . . But,
if you love that church, don't go inside. Approach,
if you must, the west door with its 14th-century
sculpture, some of the richest in Vienna ; but
go no further. Inside it is barren of all interest ;
gutted, one might say ; and the celebrated mosaic
copy of da Vinci's " Last Supper ", spread all over
the wall of the South aisle, is best left to rot unseen.
It is, as its name reveals, a monastery church, all
that remains of the monastery suppressed at the
end of the 18th century, one of Maria Theresa's
necessary acts. Since then it has been used as the
Italian church of Vienna, but a monastery church
it remains at heart, whatever may be done to it, and
its poor interior is better left in peace. When one
speaks of the Minoritenkirche one means the great
upheaving roof standing gravely removed, as it has
stood for centuries, from the antics of kings and
politicians in the meretricious hovels at its feet.

Yet just those hovels form the basis of our story.
That ancient church has nothing much to do with
it. It stands there as the only unadapted relic of the
early border days. St. Stephen's has been softened,

The Minoritenkirche

The Stefansdom

St. Michael's and the church of the Augustinians.
There are, in the ancient part of the city, two chapels
and a church dating back beyond the Minoritenkirche, and unsoftened. But these are so lost in the
huddle of streets and lanes that they can strike no
dominating note. One of them is very beautiful,
the Church of Maria Stiegen, or Maria am Gestade,
raised up and approached by steps, as the name tells
us, above the end of the Salvatorgasse on the very
edge of that ancient fortified area of the Babenbergs.
It is notable for a tall, many-sided tower culminating
in an open-work lantern of extreme loveliness. And
then there are the two chapels attached to the old
city hall, or Rathaus, one early, the other late gothic,
the last softened, moreover, by a renaissance porch,
one of the city's few memorials of that style. But
apart from these, hidden away out of sight, there
is little enough to take the mind back to those early
days of Habsburg dominion when the rulers still
had to fight for what they held and Vienna was a
headquarters of strife. St. Stephen's, the Augus-
tine Church and St. Michael's have all been adapted
and softened by later generations. Others, which
need not trouble us, were so thoroughly rebuilt in
the 18th-century style that, for all practical purposes,
they are 18th-century churches. Only the dark out-
line of the Minoritenkirche stands unbending in the
flood of southern light. The west door of that church,
with its sculpture, belongs to the middle of the
14th century, to the first days of Habsburg. The main
fabric was completed just a century later just before
Frederick lost Vienna and all the signs showed that

the days of the Habsburgs were over. It looked like the end.

But it was not the end of the Habsburgs, only of an era. With Frederick's son, Maximilian, we find the period of St. Stephen's coming to a close. Europe is settling down for the major contests. The eternal squabbling between insignificant powers is petering out. The heavy-weights appear, and, behind the frontiers, there is space and comparative peace for living. Spain has been united bloodily by Ferdinand and Isabella. Columbus has discovered America, opening the way to richer treasures than can be found at home to those with a mind for plunder. In England the Wars of the Roses (coeval with our Habsburg squabbling) have given place to the prosperous reign of Henry VII. In France the gangster Louis XI, " the universal spider ", has pulled things together after the Hundred Years' War and gone some way towards founding that country's future greatness. Lorenzo the Magnificent has arisen in Italy, in which country burns the light which is to irradiate all Europe. Discovery is in the air : printing ; gunpowder. And in Austria, consonant with the universal tendency resisted only by the northern states of Germany, Habsburg is arising as a power. This obscure line of German nobles, forsaking their hereditary territories and now thrust back from newer conquests, is, by a combination of tenacity, opportunism and accident, to become one of those monstrous heavy-weights the first of whom already take the ring. That insignificant territory won by Rudolf, and lost by his grandson Frederick with all the appearances of finality, is to become the nucleus of the greatest European power, " the eternal counterpoise to France ". And its capital, that fortress city, Vienna, now divorced from Habsburg, now in the hands of a foreign king, Matthias Corvinus of Hungary, will develop into one of the five stars—Paris, Rome, London, Madrid, Vienna.

It is now in a state of ferment. The citizens, the craftsmen, are for the first time showing themselves as a power to be reckoned with, winning rights for themselves, a share in the government by force, choosing (the Habsburgs being away) their governors. The era when kings and nobles all over Europe were fighting each other for local power and building lofty churches for fear of God and the Pope, while the people worried along as best they could, is palpably ending. It is true that Maximilian still has to fight for his possessions, starting from Innsbruck, sweeping the invading Turk before him, and being hailed as a redeemer by the people of Vienna—that for a small beginning, the recovery of a retrograde step. Considering its proximity to Italy one might have expected the Renaissance, now at its height in that peninsula, to have touched Vienna a little sooner ; but that is to forget Vienna's peculiar situation. As the private possession of the Roman Emperor it is tied to Germany, and that is enough to keep any city back. It also faces the East.

But even in this German city that dark age is ending now. Its monuments are the gothic churches, witness in Vienna as elsewhere to a tortured, bigoted, sublime, hysterical aspiration. It is the era of the Stefansdom, and as if symbolically to round it off we find that no Austrian prince is buried in its catacombs after the middle of the 15th century ; while, standing immensely in the Thekla Choir, is Nicolas van Leyden's great monument to Frederick III, father of Maximilian, last of the Mediaeval Habsburgs.

.   .   .   .   .   .

The tale of the Middle Ages is not expressed by the epithet " dark ". One could say a good deal about the glories of that period for Vienna, and scattered throughout Austria are more great monuments to indicate the boldness of the age. If gothic architecture suggests an imagination twisted, it is also no less a witness to a virile sturdiness of purpose. There were not only warring dukes and emperors ; there were also the people—and the priests. Much beauty was created, and although by its German origin debarred from sharing the first sunshine of the Italian Renaissance, we find our city with a strong background of native art and scholarship. There was Rudolf's new university ; Albert the horticulturist was full of the new wonder of Italian mathematics ; trade was growing richer and enriching princes ; there was much artistic activity besides that enshrined in the fabrics of these churches. The sculpture of St. Stephen's is much of it of a very high order, and it sprang from native talent. In that church is the famous " Servants' Madonna ", while at Klosterneuberg, outside the limits of the city, is another Madonna in marble, which meant a great deal to later sculptors. The Court delighted in illuminated manuscripts and it was in Vienna that German panel painting had its origin. But all this was essentially German, and though the virtues of the Middle Ages found expression here as everywhere we need not dwell on them. The Babenbergs patronised the Minnesingers and Walther van der Vogelweide was honoured at their court, but it was in Southern France that the strange winter flowering was at its loveliest. The gothic arts were practised, but these too had their apogee elsewhere. The true and peculiar culture of Vienna is neither German nor Italian but something in between. It begins with Maximilian, not as a pure reflection of Italy's rebirth but rather as a reflection of the harsher Teutonic Reformation, tempered by Catholicism and the neighbourhood of Italy.

Perhaps the greatest figure of the dawning light was Michael Pacher, a painter and sculptor of South Tyrol, a German expanding in Italian warmth. In him may be seen, perhaps for the first time, the unique quality which is to irradiate so much of Austria's subsequent creation, deriving from the tension between, or the fusion of, the contrasted cultures of the north and the south. Pacher's strongest influence was not Cranach but Mantegna; he lived beside the path by which Italian brilliance had to approach Vienna. Paintings of his are in the museums there, but to see his masterpiece one must leave Vienna and go to the lakeside village of St. Wolfgang in the Salzkammergut. There, in an old gothic church painted to look like baroque, is an altar which is one of the masterpieces of the 15th century. It is, moreover, the only German winged altar still in its perfect state and still used as it was intended to be used. Both the painting and the carving were done by this extraordinary man, and in them he contrives to attain that combination of German earnestness of feeling and Italian grace and sense of form which is the Austrian contribution to our world. It seems to me a gift of extreme value, which if developed and kept pure might save the world.

In Pacher we see (at least, the present writer likes to see) the first beginnings of a long preparation, lasting two hundred years, for that astonishing florescence of Austrian art which was to transfigure Vienna and form the setting of a splendid culture.

.   .   .   .   .   .

There is, then, very little gothic in Vienna. Many visitors find this disappointing. Vienna with the mind is known to be an ancient city but the eye is not so easily convinced. By now, however, we should have seen enough to convince us and we need not bother any more about the older past. To me it is the newness of Vienna that is so attractive, not its antiquity. I have not the least intention of starting a discussion of the ethics and aesthetic of gothic ; everyone knows that the gothic cathedrals of Europe are among our rarest treasures ; no one in his senses would dream of wishing away the dreaming spires and thrusting buttresses. But it is one thing to preserve some manifestations of that

style as precious relics, quite another to live out one's
life immured in it—as is done, for instance, by the
inhabitants of many northern cities.

All through its history Vienna has been linked
with Germany, sometimes very closely, sometimes
only loosely. It could hardly have been otherwise :
the Habsburgs were German princes ; Ostmark was
a province of the German Empire ; the Austro-
German border in the region of Bavaria and Tyrol
was for centuries extremely fluid. During the early
years, the years which raised St. Stephen's as their
loftiest monument, Vienna was entirely German.
German gothic was its natural expression ; the
masons who built the towers of the Cathedral were
closely connected with Ratisbon ; sometimes the
architecture of what is now the Reich was influenced by Austria, sometimes the influence was
reversed. Vienna might have remained German for
ever. It was spared that fate by its proximity to Italy
and by the Habsburg land-lust : the subject races,
Slavonic and Italian, to say nothing of Magyar (which
is something quite by itself), enriched and refined
the German blood, and with it the German taste
and all therein entailed. While Germany was and
still is extremely parochial in all her inclinations,
Vienna has developed rapidly as a cosmopolitan
centre. Germany found an early expression in the
gothic symbolism, and ever since, save in the south,
has looked with suspicion if not rabid distaste on
anything else. Vienna shared in that early gothic
expression but later allowed herself to be moulded
by newer, lighter influences, refusing to let the past

distort the present. The climate, and notably the *Föhn*, must also have been an agent in this transformation. Hence in Vienna there is little gothic. What there is one cherishes. There is not enough to oppress one, and it is satisfactory to be reminded through those monuments that in some distant past even the Viennese were fierce and serious like the rest of us.

We have seen enough, then, to convince us that this city has a past as tortuous as any. All these rococo caperings are not the vulgar flourishes of parvenus ; they are the highly significant gestures of a people which suffered the mediaeval purge and came through into light—somewhat intoxicated by it, if you like, but at least emergent. Some have not come through at all.

You have, then, to choose between Hans Sachs and the *Rosenkavalier*. Or rather, you haven't to choose at all ; up to a point you can have them both ; they both exist. That kind of choice is impossible to make. Hans Sachs produced Bach and the Nazi party ; the *Rosenkavalier* Mozart and the Ballhausplatz—and all that happened there. This is to show that I have no intention, fundamentally, of obliterating Germany that Austria may shine. Both countries have failed ; neither, that is to say, has produced a receipt for an enduring culture and carried it into execution ; so that by that touchstone neither is any better than it should be, any more than any other country of our complex—with the bare possibility of France. But one may be granted one's preferences ; there is no suppressing the sempiternal IF—and IF all that is implicit in the culture of Vienna had had the strength to survive and develop, one feels, the present writer feels, that that city would offer a fuller life than, say, Berlin, also transcendentalised. . . . On the other hand Bach led a prosperous, bourgeois life, while Vienna left Schubert to starve—though even that may bear some looking into.

We have still a long way to go to Mozart, but we shall not linger on it overlong. Vienna is the city of baroque, rococo, stuccoed elegance, music and *savoir vivre*. From the heart of all this a few gothic spires stick up, to give an edge to the general urbanity. These spires we have accounted for, and our eyes are now claimed by the green copper dome of the Karlskirche, the richly dazzling new interiors of ancient churches, the formal brilliance of a score of splendid palaces. To understand them, nevertheless, we shall have to dwell on their background for a little longer. All this did not come with Maximilian, though it dawned with him. In the altarpiece of Michael Pacher it is easy to see, wise after the event, that Austria will produce a Mozart, not a Bach, and that those without the greatness to create a *Figaro* will express a similar yet coarser talent in some glorious architectural fantasy like the Belvedere. It took our city two hundred years to journey that road, but so little is left by the wayside that it will take us no time at all. The plant pushed through the crusted ground with the rebirth of Habsburg strength in Maximilian. The bickering of minor factions was at an end ; movements and aggressions were more spacious and deliberate; but the flower did not unfurl its petals while the clouds still menaced. The menace was the Turk. At the very close of the 17th century the Turk was finally pushed back, back from the walls of the city, those same walls which were built by the Babenbergs with Richard Lionheart's ransom money, back from Austria, from Hungary. For the first time in its history—and how late!—our city could freely breathe. It burst its gates and spread over the surrounding fields. And the men were already born who were to celebrate the new freedom by rebuilding—no longer restrained by mediaeval considerations. It all came with such a rush. For two centuries after the renaissance of Italy Vienna was confined to her walls by the necessity of keeping Asia out of Europe. No wonder, that when the pressure was at last withdrawn, there was some froth.

IV. THE HOFBURG

FOR the next two hundred years, from the end of the 15th century to the end of the 17th, the symbol of Vienna is the Hofburg, the Imperial Palace, while Vienna itself is the symbol of increasing Habsburg might. There are few monuments belonging to this period, and the most important of these are parts of the palace itself; these two centuries saw, indeed, far less native creative activity than the Middle Ages which they followed. There was a growing interest in art and things of the mind, but these were entirely under the thumb of the Habsburg rulers, who looked beyond the Austrian frontiers for life's graces, principally to Italy. It was an age, so far as Vienna was concerned, less of making than of collecting, an age of preparation for the supreme creative effort which was to start in the last quarter of the 17th century. The astonishing thing is, really, that Vienna was, when the hour came, able to rise up from beneath the dead weight of accumulated alien influences and establish a style of her own.

But although we must pay attention to this period, the period dominated by the Hofburg, from which it took its tone, we must not lose ourselves too long in it. We are, when all is said, in search of the mood of a dying culture, and the background must not be allowed to dominate. That culture, its flower, is no more symbolised by the wars of bigotry and persecution which followed the Reformation, and of which the Hofburg was, if the term is allowed, the G.H.Q., than by the gothic towers and primitive paintings and chivalrous verses of the Middle Ages. It is reflected by the outward appearance of the streets in which we move today; that is baroque, tempered by rococo, complicated by various other shades. But without the Hofburg, with all its grimness, that complex mood could never have arisen.

The whole mood, a mood of astonishing and sublime subtlety when transcendentalised, you will find in an opera by Mozart; untranscendentalised, but reflected with nostalgic accuracy, in one by Richard Strauss: *Il Nozze di Figaro* and *Der Rosenkavalier*.

The languages are significant. Mozart never wrote an opera called *Figaros Hochzeit* whatever he may have done about *Der Zauberflöte*.

In the midst of the Hofburg itself, between the Schweizerhof and the Spanish Riding School on the one hand, and the open Josefsplatz on the other, is a great ballroom known simply as the Redoutensaal. It is a late 18th-century conception, arrived at when the first impulse of baroque fantasy was exhausted and the clamour had gone from the untrammelled ebullition of high faith, when baroque, in a word, had become refined into rococo, studied, pretty and self-conscious. In this room, much as it was when

Mozart received his sparing Habsburg patronage, you may today see *Figaro* played as it might have been played in its youth. That performance you will find at once enchantment and the profoundest criticism.

It is a long hall, seating some six hundred people. To more than the height of a man the walls are covered with the finest Gobelins, and above these, against cool panelling picked out with gold, embellished with every conceivable device of gilded ornament, are long mirrors reflecting and counter-reflecting in a sort of gleaming haze all the formal elegance made dazzling by the brilliance from the crystal chandeliers suspended from the gilded ceiling. At one end there is a sort of stage, a raised platform, backed by a decorated sweep of wall which continues the line of the mouldings above the tapestries, and this is broken by a branching stair-case, scarlet-carpeted, forming a sort of balcony which is opened on to by tall double doors, high above the level of the stage. That is the setting. There are screens to suggest a room, gilt chairs for the characters to sit on; or orange-trees in green tubs to indicate a garden.

In these surroundings the intrigue is at home. It is a satire by Beaumarchais on the manners of the aristocracy of France, so soon to fall. Such manners extend to other 18th-century societies, even to that society which raised this dazzling ballroom in harmony with its purest moods, which carelessly patronised the creator of this music by which it is remembered and as carelessly let an Italian rival pull wires that Mozart might starve. Beaumarchais satirised these people with elegant ferocity. Mozart agreed to the satire, no doubt, but turned it into truth, so that it lost its cutting edge and became only a reflection, non-committal like all reflections, like all reflections posing an eternal riddle, too honest to pretend either one way or the other, too flawless to suppress the slightest trait which, distorted or eliminated, might seem to make things easier to comprehend, to applaud, to condemn. All we know is that Cherubino is a lovesick youth, a petticoat sentimentalist; that Rosina is a painted aristocrat trying to save her name from scandal; that Figaro is a glib and unscrupulous dago, for ever on the make. And so on. But Cherubino can also breathe the timid, tentative, suddenly headlong ecstasy of *Non so piu cosa son, cosa faccio*; Rosina, with all the feeling in the world, can unwind the exquisite golden strand of *Porgi amor, qual che ristoro*. And the Viennese of the 18th century could, up to a point, applaud these things, even though their emotion did not extend to care of its creator.

In this opera, which is probably the most perfect expression of comedy the world has ever seen, we have, as in Verdi's *Falstaff* and one or two others, a clearer glimpse than usual of that counterpoint of moods, unobtainable by any other art, which makes the operatic form potentially the richest. Its qualities are unique, in degree if not in kind. Cherubino *is* the fickle, silly sentimentalist, but he is also the solemn, simple gravity of *Voi che sapete*,

the swift, dipping, soaring ardour of *Non so piu*. The
genius of Mozart has made him all these things at
once, and more besides. I know of no other art
whereby this miracle could be achieved with com-
parable clarity and by straightforward means. A
great deal may be suggested in painting. The
" White Gilles " of Watteau contains so many frag-
ments of the truth in such a bewildering array that
facing it we know ourselves to be in the presence
of the flawless mirror which offers, if only we can
fathom it, the reflection of the whole ; but here the
effect depends a good deal on symbolism ; it must :
and the symbol, even in its subtlest and most
delicate form, can be no more than an approxima-
tion, a reflection, faintly refracted, of a reflection.
In opera, in the opera of Mozart, the symbol is
superseded ; truth strikes straight at the heart,
short-circuiting the resistance of the mind. In words
alone a great deal may be said, but the blinding
moment is denied. That intensity of vision resulting
from the simultaneous flash of many facets is pre-
cluded by the element of time : the light is there,
but it is white light seen through a prism, split up
into its component colours, each separate and refined.
Music itself, absolute and unfettered by any physical
tie, offers, as nothing else can, the truth of our
dreams. But that is not the whole truth ; our mortal
truth is ignored. For a brief spell we may forget it ;
we may even persuade ourselves that it has no
validity ; yet when the orchestra rises to its feet and
packs its instruments that dream is broken. But
when the final chords of *Figaro* are drowned in the

H

applause no dream is lost : we do not pass nakedly
from one world to another; the world of Parisian
intrigue, fused with the world of Mozart's music,
is the world we inhabit; it is our own world which,
for a few hours, we have seen with eyes slightly
superhuman, the vision causing in us an agony of
tenderness.

To say that Cherubino is Cherubino, while *Voi
che sapete* is Mozart alone, is neither here nor there.
That the music is Mozart nobody will deny; yet
Mozart was also Cherubino—and Figaro. And the
Almavivas ; and all the rest. It comes to the same
thing whichever way we look at it. The miracle is
of course achieved by the close and palpable juxta-
position of what is and what might have been; by
the earth-bound characters before our eyes linked
with the music, irresponsible and free as air, by
words from everyday life.

In our rococo ballroom, with the old intrigue of
Beaumarchais unfolding itself in its natural setting,
the flashing, crystal-lighted ballroom which we
may penetrate only because the society which called
it into being is now dead, this miracle achieved by
art can affect us more acutely than is possible in any
theatre built as such. This is not due to sentimental
associations of the more obvious kind. As far as I
know none of Mozart's operas was ever played in the
precincts of this palace. Certainly *Figaro* was written
for a theatre as a theatre-piece. As far as I know
Mozart never so much as set foot in this ballroom,
built to the satisfaction of his Queen, though he may

very well have done so. It was not here but at the
new palace of Schönbrunn that he promised to
marry Marie Antoinette—she having picked up the
bewigged and powdered prodigy of five who had
fallen on the slippery parquet. It is simply that here
the play is actual, while in a theatre it is not. It may
have been in the theatre of Mozart's day, when the
characters on the stage were plainly extensions of
the men and women in the auditorium, right down
to details of dress and mannerism. Today, however,
we go to the opera for an evening's artificial entertainment; for a few hours we sit watching a fancy-
dress play about fancy-dress people. The music,
instead of deepening the sense of reality, heightens
the artificiality. Even the theatre building is a fancy-
dress affair, though of a different period: it is possible
that 19th-century patrons of the opera felt at home
in the red-plush show-case with its tasteless em-
bellishments in brass and gilding; but as for us—
the moment we enter it we step from actuality into
the peculiar world of the theatre, and anything
presented there, unless reflecting the manners of
our age, becomes at once a raree show, a titillation
for the eyes and ears. As an extreme example of
this process we need only glance at Gay's poor
Beggar's Opera, which now, thanks entirely to the
sterilising properties of the " theatre ", is a charming entertainment for suburban schoolgirls.

But the Redoutensaal in the Hofburg in Vienna
brings Mozart so close that you could touch him.
The setting, the words, the music, are all of a piece.
Our clothes do not matter. The scene would be

happier for a few uniforms among us, a touch of jewellery here and there; but their absence is not a serious matter. The charm of the tapestried walls is potent enough to subdue the time illusion, that fatal bar to a proper sympathy with what is past, whether in Mozart or Shakespeare or anybody else. And so one is close to this performance, a part of it, almost. It is seen not only as the most beautiful entertainment in the world, but also as a work of art of infinite profundity.

Meanwhile we have our mood, which we are seeking ; the mood of Vienna, transcendentalised. It is here, caught on this stage, fixed eternally by a man of amazing gifts who did not fully share it, reflected somewhat by the setting; and we are also in that setting. Put rationally, I suppose, it is a mood of *après nous le déluge* ; but I see no point in trying to rationalise such matters. It is, at any rate, the mood of the first splendour of decadence ; and the beginning of decay is, for exquisiteness, the supremest moment. It is not, that first beginning, a moment of decline ; on the contrary, it is the last, intoxicated, soaring flight of a spirit from which the stamina has gone. The first years of the decadence of a great society may be compared in their overreaching brilliance with the inspired and febrile eagerness of a consumptive. There is the same tell-tale eager flush.

That flush is plain on the cheeks of the characters in the play, but it is absent from the music. Mozart belonged to the decadence, but he was not a part of it ; that is his greatness. In the features of the char-

acters of Beaumarchais and da Ponte we perceive
the imminence of decline; in the music itself we
do not. This society characterised here has reached
an air too rarefied for normal man to breathe for
long. At the very moment when the nurtured plant
breaks into bloom it is found to be over-nurtured.
The cultivation has been too intensive. The stamina
is weakened; mankind must recoil to leap again,
but there is no guarantee that next time the leap
will be higher, or even as high. That Mozart was
somehow aware of the spiritual crisis of his age can
hardly be doubted. To some extent every artist must
be coloured by the mood of the age he lives in; if
he is not, one of the many requisites of a work of
art cannot be supplied: that is, the tension arising
from the simultaneous contemplation of what is
with what might have been. That preoccupation,
sentimental if ever anything was, is indispensable;
even the artist of the sanest, most gruffly matter-of-
fact reputation cannot do without it. The work of
Mozart is not as *healthy* as the work of Bach, but it
is no less sane. *Figaro* is as sane as *Candide*; Voltaire
as sentimental as Mozart. The works of both these
men depend on the same indispensable tension.
Voltaire tried to hide his sentimental approach, from
himself as well as from others; Mozart did not, that
is all. Bach lived in a healthier age than Mozart,
Mozart in a healthier age than Schubert, Schubert
in a healthier age than Schumann. But healthiness
is an animal quality existing apart from mental
development and balance, though often getting
intertwined with it. As for sanity—it would, I

think, be possible to argue that Schumann was as sane as Bach. Schumann, we know, had himself certified at his own request and died in an asylum ; Bach was a comfortable organist of a cathedral city, wearing a full-bottomed wig and rearing an extensive progeny. Just as Shakespeare would have seemed a lunatic in Dryden's day, so Dryden, cast up and back among the Elizabethans, would have seemed no less insane. Insanity is not a constant. Even the conception of health leads us nowhere in particular. If *Kreisleriana* is less healthy than the *Jupiter*, and if this is less healthy than the *Goldberg Variations* the differences between these works are dwarfed by the gulf between them all and " Sumer is icumen in ".

As for the ages themselves—have we any right to generalise about their relative states of mind ? To us the 18th century is likely to seem sane, the 19th somewhat mad. It may be so, but there is no telling: the sanity of the 18th century could with the utmost ease be made to appear as a colossal and complacent megalomania, causing men to delude themselves into the conviction that a sense of form and order could be imposed by man on life; while the romantic fallacy of the succeeding years might be seen in another light, as the bringing of a sense of proportion and modesty to bear on human problems, the surrender to the current of the turbulent stream. It is not only difficult to generalise about these things; it is impossible.

Mozart, perhaps, was a little mad because he was so sane; he was certainly abnormal. His music is

full of strength; it is fertile. And this went against
the spirit of his age and doubtless caused, as much
as court intrigue, the Viennese preference over him
for Salieri. The Viennese of that day were losing
their spiritual strength, which they have never
since recovered; and in Mozart we find the mood of
our city, transcendentalised, because in him we find
all the surface wonders of a high culture together
with an inner strength. In other words we have a
miracle: the perfect, or so it seems to us, expression
of sophistication allied with a virility absent as a rule
from it. The strength is in the roots, in the stem,
if you like, not in the flower. Mozart managed to
impart it to the flower so that it lives for ever, a
sublime witness to what might have been. Or so it
seems to us. . . . That qualification is necessary:
with this perspective, with a century and a half
between us and those times, we doubtless overlook
things. For us the miracle exists. In so far as we can
apprehend that culture, Mozart has fixed it. But to
his own contemporaries it may have seemed otherwise. What seems to us a perfect reflection may have
seemed to them no reflection at all. The phrase of
the Emperor Joseph on the first night of this opera,
Figaro (" You must admit, my dear Mozart, there
are a great many notes "—and Mozart's answer :
" But not one too many, Sire "), may indicate a gulf
not merely running between genius and the common
man, but also between the man of his age and the
man not quite of it. So, for the Viennese, the miracle
may not have existed. For us it does. In the more
superficial charms of Mozart's music we find re-

flected with sufficient perfection all the excellencies
and elegance and charm of that most brilliant of all
fins de siècles. That flavour we may still find about
the city today—for, since then, nothing has happened. Nothing.

That mood of sophisticated elegance is the only
mood to justify the construction of great cities. To
live in a city one must turn the back on many
delights, advantages, enduring virtues. To replace
the naturalness and leisuredness of country life one
must, it seems to me, demand something very high
in the way of compensation, and this can only come
in the form of an intensive, artificial culture. At the
close of the 18th century we find this state of affairs
attained in many European cities, perhaps in Vienna
above all; and of all cities Vienna has contrived to
preserve, even to the present barren day, something
of that mood. At the turn of the 19th century the
volatile Hermann Bahr, for long imagining himself
and his companions supremely young and forward-
looking, had to admit that all his life had been spent
in the age of baroque : " I mistook the dying afterglow for the first flush of dawn ". That afterglow
was so sustained and long drawn out, painting the
sky with such ceaselessly changing harmonies of
colour, that those with a horizon bounded by it may
be excused for their delusion ; although, looking
back, it is hard to see what hope for a vital future
could be found in the small perfection of von
Hoffmanstal. He and Schnitzler and some others
remained in Vienna to see the old world out ;
others, who believed that elsewhere in Europe there

Schönbrunn

The Gardens, Schönbrunn

was still recuperative power, had to leave. Vienna today, as in the last days of the Habsburgs, still lives in the era of rococo. There we may still find the relic of a city culture, a relic not confined, as in Paris, to certain quarters, but faintly colouring the whole. London has lost all pretensions to such a culture ; Paris is losing it; but Vienna, so long as it exists, will, I think, to a degree, retain it. The city, the great city, is one of the manifestations of our culture, which is dying fast. The city state of Athens falls into another category ; there the city was the state, not merely its headquarters. The true city culture was something new, which is now already dead, although, as we have said, in Vienna it lingers on. In the music of Mozart we find its idealisation, which was never attained save in imagination; and that is fitting, for the city culture alone made the music of Mozart possible, or much of it. Indeed, as far as I can see, the major if not the sole aesthetic contribution on the part of our culture to the rise of civilisation generally (I mean that civilisation of all mankind, comprehending a thousand cultures, which through millennia slowly stirs and heaves and bubbles, now lifting a little, now suddenly collapsing, now lifting again, this time a little further, for all the world like a slowly rising yeasty mass) is the art of concerted music, including opera. For it seems probable that the culture which was born with the Renaissance, for all its artistic glories, has been more for science than for art, with the music of the decadence playing a curious rôle which we may glance at later.

The sunshine of a great culture is a fleeting thing; nothing brings home more sharply the swift transcience of human effort imposed on the eternal sameness of life itself. One may compare it to a day of festival. For months the preparations have been going on, drawing greater and greater numbers actively into the orbit of the event, though many times their number stand outside it. As the day approaches it is heralded by unfamiliar sights, by streets displaying bunting, by carriages rehearsing for the grand procession, by strangers swarming in from far and near. There is in the air, shared even by those who stand outside the preparations, a feeling of expectancy, a sense of common purpose temporarily breaking down the individual barriers called into being by the law of self-preservation; within the hearts of millions there is a stirring of emotions unfamiliar and larger than those called into action by the life of everyday. The individual I is temporarily surprised by the sense that it is not the absolute centre of the universe; that place of honour belongs, it seems, by rights to something greater and above the ego, but vaguely apprehended, and symbolised by the day. And as the day draws very close—it may be a royal jubilee, or a coronation —all eyes are turned, as it were, both outwards and upwards. There is a power in all these millions touched into life by this common preoccupation with something outside the daily run of earning daily bread ; and, ironically, this immense power is out of all proportion to the stimulus which has aroused it from its sleep and yet is centred solely on that stimulus. However, the procession starts. There is a sudden roll of drums, a blaze of colour. Those who have waited so long are finally transported. This is the great event, the aim and purpose of so much work and waiting; this is the moment of our lives. But it is passing. It does not stand still. A gold and scarlet uniform, worn once in a lifetime, taken out and furbished for days to this end, appears and is gone in a flash. Those plumes which brighten our vision do not stay. They give place to others, we know, but we also know that soon there will be no others. And almost before the pageant has begun the climax is approaching, is here, is gone, the fabulous coach of gold, witness of fairyland, sways past and is away. That is what we have waited hours to see; that is what thousands have actively prepared for for so long, and it is all over in a flash—a mounted rearguard, then nothing more. A thin shaft of brilliance cutting across grey years. The moment does not stay. But perhaps it is those months of silent preparation that count—those and the afterglow. . . . And that, enormously magnified, is the progress of a culture. After years of brooding there is a stirring, after years of stirring a sudden flash of brilliance, and then, another, and another, until radiance is everywhere; and even in that moment the first lights are extinguished, and the process goes on, but the waning less gradual and more sudden than the waxing, until only a few points glimmer here and there.

So it has been with Vienna.

The years between the dawn of the Renaissance and the flowering of Austrian baroque, those two centuries linking the Middle Ages with the modern city, were full of a stirring, but they have left few concrete relics. As we have said, the influences were foreign. Under Maximilian, who favoured German talent, there was a liveliness of artistic effort throughout all Southern Germany and Austria, an ebb and flow across the borders of provinces and duchies, resulting in the forming of the Danube style. Cranach was its leader, but Michael Pacher had not lived in vain. At Innsbruck we find the Emperor's own tomb, also German, an extraordinary collective monument with twenty-eight bronze figures of varying quality which it took a generation to complete. Dürer too owed much to Maximilian, who paid him an annual pension, which was continued by the Emperor Charles V, first and greatest of the Spanish Habsburgs, on the master's return to Italy; so to Charles, I suppose, who so loved Titian that he sat for three portraits for him, exclaiming that he was thrice immortalised, it may be said that we owe the " Madonna of the Cut Pear ", the " Portrait of a Young Venetian Lady ", and, most marvellously of all, the " Adoration of the Trinity ", that masterpiece of masterpieces, tiny in size, infinite in spatial suggestiveness, with clouds of angels *floating* in the air.

But all this was extra-Vienna, as it were, having to do with the Empire as a whole rather than with our city. That was still a fortress and but recently won back by Habsburg. It was not dead, however.

Although it contributed little, it was something of a centre. It had its music; it was Maximilian who founded the celebrated Hofkapelle, that most perfect of boys' choirs, now housed in the chapel of the Burg having taken Haydn and Schubert as pupils in its stride. But there was little native creation. That was to come later when England, Flanders, France and finally North Germany had each played its part as the conservatory of Europe. Painting, after the decline of the Danube school, became a matter for Italy, and architecture with it. To that we owe our present-day Vienna. How complete was to be the Italian hold on Austrian art may be seen from the odd remaining renaissance memorials in Vienna and elsewhere, in the Schweizertor of the Hofburg, in the marvellous Porcia castle at Spital in south Carinthia, above all at Salzburg in that perfect expression of early Italian baroque, Solari's marble cathedral of the early 17th century, in the purest Italian style imaginable. That prepares us for what is to come, though nobody could guess from that alone how ardently the country was to take baroque to her heart and mould it into an image of herself.

Meanwhile the Habsburgs were prospering. The local provinces, those which form the republic of today, were consolidated by Maximilian. Marriages were being arranged, marriages which somehow linked the old age with the new. For although the reign of Maximilian means the end of the Middle Ages, he himself was a mediaeval character. " The Last of the Knights " he was called, and although he patronised the arts and sciences he was above all a fighting man, which was as well for Habsburg. In his person was still seen the flame of chivalry and he loved to risk his life in single combat; and with these qualities of gallantry and curiosity he combined a reckless temper which engaged him in undertakings far too great for him, or perhaps for his means; he squandered money, of which he had little enough, and to satisfy his ambitions and his needs was forced to take to begging. This aspect of him spoils the picture of a romantic figure, a man who in happier circumstances might have combined the virile qualities of a vanishing age with the eager questing of the new. Filled with a fire for the temporal glory of his family he yet mortified himself in death, causing his teeth to be pulled out and broken and burnt, and with them the hair of his head; his body, after public exposure, was to be put in a sack of quicklime and finally buried in a damask-covered coffin beneath the altar of the chapel in his Neustadt palace, so that the officiating priests should spurn his heart. That was Maximilian, the last of the knights, or Maximilian the Moneyless, whichever way you look at it. At any rate, a mediaeval figure.

But by his first marriage with Mary of Burgundy, daughter of Charles the Bold and Isabella of Bourbon, he brought into the family an alien and more delicate strain. A most beautiful and accomplished princess, she patronised the arts of every kind and bore two legendary children before she died, unnecessarily, as the result of a fall from her horse when riding, her leg receiving an injury which her modesty forbade her to have attended. These children were Margaret of Austria and Philip the Fair. Both seem to have owed less to their father than their mother. It was Margaret who, first betrothed to the dauphin of France, later voyaged to Spain to marry the only son of Ferdinand and Isabella, a delicate and sensitive youth who died three years later. And this Margaret, a Habsburg by name, nearly wrecked in a fearful storm, wrote a couplet which she hung round her neck at the hour of greatest peril :

> Ci-gît Margot la gente demoiselle,
> Qu'eut deux maris, et si mourut pucelle.

One should remember this, when oppressed by the cloddishness of later Habsburgs. The blood which produced that spirited farewell was also in their veins. It is a good thing, too, to remember the great bravery with which Marie Antoinette went to death. In fact this astonishing and heavy-handed family seems to have possessed some quality of excellence which shone forth only in moments of irrevocable disaster. Perhaps it was the incongruous fatalism which links the vague incompetence of the Emperor Frederick III and his recipe for supreme felicity with the short-sighted narrowness of Franz Josef, whose capacity for forgetting, suddenly and utterly, a goal irrevocably denied him upon which he had set his heart, seems in many ways so enviable. Perhaps it was something finer. At any rate, several Habsburgs faced their ends with admirable composure.

Margaret of Austria lived, but not as Queen of Spain. The succession passed to Philip—handsome, indolent, casual, gifted, but all too easy to himself ; that Philip who married Mad Joanna, the hideous daughter of Their Catholic Majesties, died young, and was carted about in his coffin by his imbecile spouse, who allowed no woman near it and viewed the decomposing body day by day. This pair produced two children, two sons of considerable parts. It is a wonder they were not lunatics or cretins ; instead they were the Emperors Charles V and Ferdinand I. But perhaps it is not too fanciful to see in the afflictions of so many of their descendants, in the morbid mania which grew into the hearts and minds of so many later Habsburgs, the fruit of that evil marriage of the gay and pleasant son of the warrior German king and his gifted Burgundian princess with the degenerate daughter of a degenerate stock which had flared into a final, appalling splendour in the character of Isabella of Castile. Mad Joanna cannot have been a comfortable forebear.

For the greater part of their lives her children resisted the infection, but the melancholy colour of Charles's later years must be, at any rate in part, attributed to her. It was an un-Habsburgian end when that great figure who had once sacked Rome reigned himself to making clocks and mechanical toys of an ingenuity which procured for him a magician's reputation, and finally, almost in a frenzy, gave himself up to self-mortifications of the cruellest sort, turning his back entirely on that world which he had loved to dominate. There was nothing of Habsburg in that, but there will be something of Habsburg in it for the future. The cause of aggrandisement has much to answer for. The Habsburgs were early noted for using marriage to increase their properties, fighting for the most part only to keep what they had won by statesmanship. There is a sarcastic little Latin tag about this practice, attributed to Matthias Corvinus, the Hungarian king who took Vienna from the woolly-minded Frederick; but one wonders whether the nation suffered less harm through horrible marriages than it would have done by shedding blood in wars of conquest.

However, Charles and Joanna are beyond our orbit. The ruler of Austria was Charles's younger brother, Ferdinand, who, though built on a lesser scale, was a better balanced man. He died sane, but the fatal fever was said to have been brought on by worry and distress at his inability to heal the violent quarrels of the Church. He was the first Austrian Habsburg to count as a world power. For a grandson of the Catholic Ferdinand and Isabella he seems to have been a man of singular religious tolerance, although all his troubles with Bohemia, which led to the Bloody Diet of Prague, were due to the Catholic bigotry of the time, which inevitably found some prominence in his character. Born at Alcala de Henares and brought up in Spain, he was at an early age despatched to the Netherlands by his elder brother Charles, who was somewhat jealous of his popularity. There he had the advantage of being

I

educated according to a plan drawn up by Erasmus, with whom he for ever after corresponded. Receiving from his brother Charles the German possessions of the Habsburgs for his own use (Charles, having all but turned Spain against him by his neglect of that country during his extensive excursions throughout the length and breadth of his dominions, at last decided that the whole Habsburg property was too much for one man to manage, and settled finally in Spain), he was soon able to add to these the kingdoms of Bohemia and Hungary as a result of the politic marriage arranged for him by his grandfather, Maximilian, with Anne of Bohemia, to whose lot the countries fell when Lewis, her brother, died. In this transaction we have some insight into the decency and astuteness of Ferdinand, for he did not insist on his rights but demanded an election. His position was confirmed and all should have been set for a prosperous and expansive reign. But what with the Hungarians and the Turks, whose constant belligerency made the tenure of the Crown of Hungary scarcely more than nominal, and what with the religious troubles of his day, his life was frittered away in constant fighting, and the gifts which were his had inadequate fruition, although he never lost his interest in scholars and men of letters. In this Ferdinand, it seems to me, we see for the first time the blighting influence on an otherwise fair mind of the so-called Christian Faith, invented with such fine shrewdness by the Church of Rome and distorted so obscenely by Spanish maniacs and holy perverts. And yet, as we shall see in a moment, the

issue is never a clear one, for, without the Spanish
lunacy, operating in and through the Habsburgs,
great areas of Europe would have become a province
of the Sultan's empire. . . . However, for the good
Catholic, Vienna must have been a pleasant and
fairly cultivated place under Ferdinand I. He was
at any rate the first modern Habsburg to govern
from the Hofburg, and it was he who started the
remodelling of that ancient stronghold, commission-
ing the lovely renaissance work of the Schweizerhof, called after the Swiss mercenaries employed as
palace guards, including the Schweizertor which
survives for us today.

Under his son, who followed him, life must have
been still more pleasant. This was the second Maximilian, who seems to have combined in his person
most of the virtues and few of the faults of a mild
and benevolent despot, but who is despised by many
historians for his failure to provide them with the
customary charnel-house of strife and bloodshed on
which to drape their hackneyed phrases. The main
object of Maximilian II was to govern peacefully
so that his personal lands and the Empire as a whole
might have time to consolidate their positions. All
his tributaries and subjects seem to have got on well
with him, and much is to be said for a man who
could earn the praises, simultaneous and apparently
sincere, of Germans, Hungarians, Bohemians, Austrians, Catholics and Protestants alike. He was the
first (with the possible exception of Albert, who died
of eating melons) and the last of all the Habsburgs
to achieve such universal popularity. He made,

however, one terrible mistake, and that the most seemingly innocent imaginable. In 1548 he married his cousin Mary, a 16th-century Spanish Catholic princess—a dangerous lunatic, in other words, or a pillar of the Faith, which ever way you care to look at it. If you believe in the accidental theory of history, which so many seem to love (*i.e.* that if James Watt had happened to leave the room on urgent business just before the kettle boiled we should be travelling in stage-coaches to this day), you will doubtless see in this inauspicious celebration the direct cause of the Thirty Years' War, the resultant rise of the Hohenzollerns, the subsequent war of 1914, the unsettlement of values consequent on this, culminating in the abdication of Edward VIII of England. If, on the other hand, you take the fatalistic view, preferring to preserve your sanity, and feel satisfied that the war to save democracy would have started without the intervention of the daughter of Charles V and that the steam-engine would still have been invented had Watt been born blind, you will modestly record that the installation of this Mary, a most accomplished woman, as consort of the Emperor and mother of future Habsburg rulers, at the most slightly accelerated the fermenting process which was suddenly to explode and cause a universal conflagration (I mean the Thirty Years' War, not the late Great one). She accelerated this because, in spite of her husband's tolerant spirit (or perhaps because of it?), she had complete charge of his children's upbringing. When this woman returned to Spain, a widow, her first remark was an exclamation of delight at being once more in a land where there was not a single heretic. She saw to it that her children took after her.

The most important of these were Rudolf, Matthew and Maximilian. The first two became Emperors, the third did not, but he had the guardianship of the wretched Ferdinand II.

Rudolf, as far as one can tell, without that Spanish taint (which his grandfather had received only slightly and his father not at all, but which, through his father's marriage, had been doubled), would have been an amiable if ineffectual monarch. Even as things were he was the first of the Habsburgs to show a passionate understanding of the arts, and with this he combined an intellectual liveliness rare among the members of his family and taking one back to the days of Albert the Horticulturist. But like Albert, and with less excuse (the Middle Ages were long left behind), his science was three parts magic. He patronised Tycho Brahe and Kepler in their true research, but he also fell a victim to the astrological pretensions of the former, whom he especially esteemed. This plus the Spanish blood, was indeed his total undoing. He became persuaded that his life would be taken by one of his own family and became a recluse of the most morbid order, his religious mania and his fear of death mingling to form the most miserable of complexes. He degenerated so far that his palace in Prague, where he had taken up his residence, was converted by his command into something like a prison with covered communicating passages between the various parts so that the king need never show himself. Always indolent and lazy, except where his religion was at stake, he gradually shut himself off from all government of his lands, which got into a chaotic state, and it is not surprising to find his energetic younger brother, Matthew, scheming to bring about his abdication. In due course and with much upset Rudolf was set aside ; and Matthew, whose energy had heralded an auspicious reign, did little but keep the throne warm, as it were, for Ferdinand, a member of the Tyrol branch of the family. Ferdinand, though by no means the next in the succession, was chosen to save the Austrian Habsburgs from extinction ; neither Rudolf, nor Matthew, nor his brother Maximilian, had male issue or any prospect of it ; all were ageing, and for all three of them to die without any provision for the future would have been to invite the claims of the Spanish branch to the Austrian throne. But although Ferdinand's elevation was uneasily contrived the curious thing is that the Bohemians, who could have put their foot down, acquiesced to it, thereby ensuring the supremacy of one who was to be their cruellest scourge. Why they allowed Ferdinand to succeed unquestioned is something of a mystery, for already in his own provinces he had shown himself a militant Catholic of the most rabid kind. One of his youthful acts, for instance, was to order all who would not be converted to his faith to leave his lands, and the virulence of his temper is shown by the fact that Protestants formed two-thirds of his subjects. Those who stood by their principles and left were replaced with good Catholics imported from Wallachia. And Ferdinand was not to rest content until he had applied the same principles of government throughout the whole of the German lands, stopping only at the Baltic, and only there after badly burning his fingers.

The whole of his reign was shadowed by that fearful reversion to barbarity which historians have dignified with the name of the Thirty Years' War. To begin with it was a straight fight between Catholicism and Protestantism, between the Catholic League headed by the Imperial power and the Protestant Union headed by Bohemia and Bavaria. And at the start the Catholics nearly lost ; the Bohemians reached the walls of Vienna and Ferdinand was saved only by a miracle. But Right, as usual, proved itself inept when it came to a question of organisation. The Bohemians had started off in excellent and spirited fashion with the striking act known as the Defenestration of Prague, when, egged on by Count Thurn, the head of the Protestant Estates, the Bohemian delegates at a council between the Protestants and the Catholics threw two of the Imperial Councillors out of the window at the ancient castle of Prague, the Kralovski Hrad ; but that lack of unity which seems to be an inevitable characteristic of all comparatively liberal-minded movements—for the simple and unescapable reason that to be a dissenter in one particular involves a certain proclivity to dissension generally—soon made itself felt, and the forces which Count Thurn could raise were soon as nothing before the Imperial

Catholics banded together by unspeculative simple-
ness of mind and directed by a general of genius out
for personal glory. At the battle of the White
Mountain in 1619 the Bohemian Protestants were
broken.

It is difficult, if not impossible, to get at the
rights and wrongs of this affair which ended in
the crushing of Bohemia. One naturally blames the
fearful intolerance of the Catholic Imperialists, but
the Protestants themselves were not at that time
models of open-mindedness ; they persecuted, when
they had the chance, not only the Catholics but also
each other—Calvinists, that is to say, persecuted
Lutherans, and so on. And Count Thurn, who at
first sight appears somewhat as a reckless martyr-
hero, was not the simplest of religious saints but
a man of restless and intriguing temperament of
the kind that is lost unless it can stir up trouble.
Once, however, the original purpose of the Austrians
was achieved (and how crushingly and finally it was
achieved may be adduced from the fact that from
the day of the fatal battle on the White Mountain
outside Prague until the inauguration of the Czecho-
Slovakian Republic in 1918, for three centuries
almost to a year, Bohemia, which had an ancient and
stubborn culture, ceased utterly to exist), Ferdinand,
instead of desisting and trying to restore an equi-
librium, turned on Bavaria and the Palatinate from
motives of revenge and greed, for the Bohemians
had put up the Elector Palatine as king in opposition
to him—Frederick, a Calvinist and a son-in-law of
James I of England, who would not support him

for fear of offending Spain, with whom he was trying to negotiate a marriage. Once, then, Ferdinand
had wantonly extended the original theatre of the
war, the rights and wrongs are evident enough, and
Ferdinand, with his barbaric but astonishingly able
general, Tilly, became a sort of demoniac scourge of
Central Europe and a death's head to its struggling
culture. Sweeping all before him in a fantastic cam-
paign of bigotry and greed, its sordidness relieved
by a solitary streak of romance in the personality
and dreams of his second general of genius, Wallenstein, at one time it seemed that Protestantism
would be utterly wiped out of Europe and the
Habsburg hegemony secured from the Adriatic to
the Baltic. His opponents were paralysed by the
invincibility of his generals, the boldness of his
plans and the unspeakable brutality of the Imperial
forces, which, culminating in the atrocities of
Tilly's sack of Magdeburg, entirely puts in the shade
even the barbarities of 20th-century Russia, Germany
and Spain. Nothing reveals the boundless ambition
of Ferdinand—ambition of the kind which, ruthlessly
pursued, has a hypnotic effect on all who stand in
its way—more than the attempt to establish a navy
in the Baltic, threatening the Scandinavian lands.
This project, which was actually put in hand by
Wallenstein, had about it a Napoleonic recklessness
and logic which, were it not obscured by the evil
of the war to which it was incidental, might have
earned for Ferdinand the reputation of a hero.

But the evil was unpardonable, and the hero of
this war is Gustavus Adolphus, the Protestant king

of Denmark, who, roused at length to action by the shrill hysteria of Ferdinand, rose with deliberation and advanced, slowly and with the invulnerable momentum of a steam-roller, towards the south; and although at Lützen he was killed he had Leipzig behind him and Lützen itself was won, and Habsburg had shot its bolt.

The war did not end with the death of Gustavus Adolphus, far from it. It outlasted the life of Ferdinand, and the reign of his successor, Ferdinand III, a man as mild as his father had been virulent, was fully occupied in winding it up, resting his exhausted dominions, and negotiating over the Treaty of Westphalia. Far from gaining the domination over Europe which they had hoped for and expected, the Habsburgs had to sign a document which brought into being an entirely new and rival power which was to dispute their supremacy and, finally, soon after wresting it from them, drown in a vortex of its own creation, dragging down the Habsburgs with it : the Hohenzollerns of Brandenburg.

I have recounted with regrettable inadequacy the history of these years from Maximilian to Ferdinand III not by any means for its own sake but to give some indication of the scene of which Vienna was the focus. The rise of Vienna as a major cultural centre did not begin until the middle of the 17th century, which, compared with Paris and London, was extremely late. The major causes of this retarded growth and the then extraordinarily swift and delicate flowering—*bolting* is the horti-

culturist's word—are to be found in that sad and
bloody story. While England was slowly, deliberately
maturing, Vienna was distracted : first the tender
plant which had emerged in the comparative
warmth afforded by the reigns of Ferdinand I and
Maximilian II was arrested by the blighting misrule
of Rudolf, then utterly scarified by the cold darkness
which descended during that interminable war.
Vienna was already behind the times, as we have
seen, largely owing to the Turk, and the Turk was
once more at her gates in the early days of Ferdinand
I. Nor was he ever far away until finally crushed
by the Peace of Karlowitz in 1699. In a word, what
with the Turks and the more self-righteous of the
Habsburgs, Vienna did not get a chance.

I said, earlier on, echoing Archdeacon Coxe, that
our city's major troubles sprang from her position
as a border city and a bulwark against the East ;
that this is mainly true everyone will agree, but
what of the gratuitous aggressiveness of the Thirty
Years' War? Even that, it seems to me, is part of
the same problem. If we are to thank the Habsburgs
for keeping Asia out of Europe we must also be
prepared to accept, perhaps, if not to condone, the
inevitability of campaigns of religious persecution
inside Europe on their part. I am not excusing
Ferdinand II ; although he was a good father of
his family, replete with private and domestic virtues,
and although in adversity he showed an admirable
stoicism, he remains, and must remain, one of the
blackest figures of our history. But if I am not excusing him as an individual what I am doing is to

suggest the inevitability of some such apparition in
that quarter. The Habsburgs held the Turks ; we
are all, I imagine, grateful to them for that service ;
but their main prop and inspiration in that weary
and interminable struggle was, besides self-interest,
not the Christian land of France nor the Christian
land of England, but the abstract Catholic Faith.
Ottoman was a colossal, an all but irresistible power.
It is to be questioned whether any European monarch
upheld only by motives of self-interest, however
strong these might have been (and in the Habsburgs
they were strong enough), could have sustained the
duel for so long, and ultimately triumphed. In other
words a fanatic religious faith was *necessary* in these
Habsburgs as a stay ; and if we value a Europe free
from Sultans we must be grateful for the strength
of that faith. What then ? . . . For fanaticism is not
a quality that can be controlled, switched on when
required, and switched off when it has done some
special service. Terrible as it is, it is also only human
that this fanaticism should find an expression in
fury against heretics as well as unbelievers. . . . You
cannot, in short, have a family sustained by a
necessary religious ardour without finding it, once
in a way, running amok. And thus, to take sugges-
tion a small stage further, even those unpleasant
Spanish marriages, which doubled the Habsburgs'
holy zeal, are seen to have their place. They retarded the development of Austria (which, however,
in Turkish hands, would not have developed at all) ;
they are largely responsible, indirectly, for the softness of the Viennese today ; but undeniably they

contributed to the salvation of Christendom—for what it has been worth.

The softness of the Viennese, their willingness to resign themselves to every powerful evil as irremediable, their gaiety masking a sort of chronic despair or hopelessness, their lack of intellectual tenacity, their attitude (which does not go as deep as many think) that nothing is worth the trouble of dying for—all these qualities being the obverse of many of their finest and most endearing characteristics—this has been attributed before, and must be attributed, to the scourge of Ferdinand II, which itself, as I have suggested, was occasioned by the proximity of the unbelieving East. We have already observed that this Ferdinand, as a young man, rid his lands of all Protestants who put principle above personal advantage : those who thought their homes were worth a Mass stayed on ; those who did not had to go. And that was soon the situation in Vienna and throughout the Austrian dominions. Many of the finest spirits were expelled, never to return, and the civic fibre was correspondingly weakened. Bound up with the same process, too, is the principle of the Patriots for Me, which may be said to have begun with Ferdinand, but which persisted until the end of the Habsburg tenure. Vienna, though the seat of an emperor, was only the capital of a tiny country ; through the centuries it relied for new blood on Bohemians, Poles, Hungarians and the rest ; and although among these there were many fine personalities there were many more venal ones : for those who were encouraged by the Court were precisely those who were the readiest to sever their racial affiliations, turn their backs on their native lands, and acknowledge no loyalty but to Habsburg. Many doubtless saw the highest patriotism in the support of the ruling house ; but many more saw only personal advantage. This kind of thing, the encouragement of men of shallow principle, cannot continue in a city for several hundred years without effecting a deterioration on the social fabric.

Finally, to put Vienna in its place, we should realise that during these two hundred years it was not the capital of a centralised empire, as it became a little later. It was merely the capital of Austria ; Bohemia and Hungary also had their capitals, and one emperor, the hopeless Rudolf, made Prague his capital and stayed there throughout his reign.

We should have seen enough by now to help us understand what follows, which, after the recuperative period of Ferdinand III's rule, is nothing else than the final rebirth of Vienna. We may also understand how it is that so few monuments exist to this stormy epoch between the Middle Ages and the coming of baroque. As we have said, these two hundred years in Vienna formed an age less of creation than of collection, an age of preparation. As far as building was concerned the influence was increasingly Italian, but today there is next to nothing of this period still standing in Vienna, although there are splendid relics of it in other parts of Austria. The Hofburg itself was to some extent

refashioned and enlarged. To Ferdinand's Schweizerhof, which is now at the heart of the palace, Maximilian II added the Amalienhof on the far side of
the courtyard called In der Burg and in the shadow
of the Minoritenkirche. But the mass of the palace
came later in the city's story.

Indeed, the only way to catch a reflection of the
artistic preoccupations of the rulers of this age is by
looking at the pictures which they amused themselves by collecting. The various collections, once
scattered, are now conveniently brought together
in one place.

This family had always shown an interest in
matters of art and letters ; it was expected of them.
Frederick III, in the intervals of losing his possessions and dreaming of the future greatness of his
family, had started getting together weapons and
suits of armour from the then past which served to
form a nucleus of the great collection in Vienna
which is said by those who know to be the finest
armoury in the world outside Madrid. And when
Maximilian married Anne of Burgundy, who
brought with her many rare treasures from the
Netherlands and France, the amassing process was
under way. Ferdinand I carried on on the lines laid
down, but his interest was more in men of letters
than in painters, and it was his brother Charles V
who was left to patronise the painters of the day—
perhaps because, having been brought up to rule
the world, he was more or less illiterate and
denied the pleasures of reading. But the true father
of the Imperial collections was the unhappy

Rudolf II, pottering his life away in voluntary imprisonment at Prague. His pictures and objects of art, together with nearly all of the Habsburg pictures (save the astounding collection of drawings and engravings made by various dukes and archdukes at a later date, now to be seen in the Albertina) are now housed in one of the twin sham-renaissance buildings opposite the Hofburg on the Ringstrasse (the other containing stuffed animals and birds).

Wandering through these labyrinthine galleries it is soon clear enough, even if one has no history, where the Habsburg hand lay heaviest. Apart from their own Germanic art, the Cranachs, Dürers, Griens and Holbeins, the richness of the collection, in more senses than one, is skimmed from the Netherlands and Northern Italy. Seen as a whole this museum might be a striking commentary on the tastes of the Roman emperors—if one could only find the key. As a national collection it is curious, rich, ill-balanced. The museum is called the Kunsthistorisches, or Art History, Museum ; but unless one counts the Roman and Egyptian sections (which, I suppose, one should) nothing could be more misleading. Certainly the picture section is the last place in the world to go to for a lucid cross-section of the history of European painting ; the National Gallery in London, for all its limitations, is far better suited to that purpose. In Vienna the main attraction is the extremely lavish representation of a handful of favoured artists at the cost of the neglect, or even the total omission, of as many more. The Imperial collections are to some extent supplemented by the

private collections made by various noble houses—
the Liechtensteins with their 1000 masterpieces,
the more modest Czernins and Harrachs ; but even
then, collecting seems to have broken down altogether in the 18th century, and the efforts of the
19th-century gallery to fill the gap are more pathetic
than illuminating. In any case, Van Goghs, Cézannes
and even Renoirs are out of place in Vienna. These
men all had belief. Vienna, in their age, was too
far gone to do anything but let things slide, while
they, in France, were engaged in one of those miracles
which so frequently occur to glorify a period of
decline, stimulating the etiolated nerves of Europe
electrically to new perceptions. But Vienna was
beyond their help. " Asia begins on the Landstrasse " ; and across that highway, into the heart of
a city, there had crept, all pervading, the humour
of Asiatic fatalism.

There are no important Cézannes in Vienna, but
there is a poor Van Gogh—not poor in execution,
but as one says, " poor Keats ! " ; " The Plain of
Auvers-sur-Oise " : and all it does, hanging there
in the Orangery of the Belvedere Palace, with a
handful of exiled Parisians for company, is to
emphasise, almost shockingly, all the more unpleasant qualities of our city in decline. While in
the next breath it is made to look ridiculous, because
it is in a pathetic minority, like a great hound in the
boudoir of a lap-dog.

We must forget Van Gogh if we wish to attain
our mood. There are other things in the world
besides limitless, impassioned genius. The nightin-

K

gale is not to be despised because it is not an eagle
to outsoar the mountain summits and stare un-
blinking at the sun. But intrusive images of glaciers
and frigid peaks will cause an ordered and pastoral
landscape to seem more tinsel than it is. Also, from
this cabined elegance a Mozart could arise ; and the
eagle itself took flight from the bandbox levels of
the dyke-land.

We were speaking of the Habsburgs in their new
rôle of Mæcenas. It is customary to speak of them
as connoisseurs of painting, and so some of them
doubtless were ; but to judge from the composition
of these galleries their taste was not of a catholic
and discriminating kind ; they seem, in fact, to have
taken what lay to their hand, and as much of it
as possible, without seriously looking beyond their
immediate orbit. Quite evidently the Habsburg
passion was for colour, Venetian colour at that,
colour all aglow. By comparison the Florentines are
poorly patronised. Wall after wall blazes richly with
the reds and golds of Venice : Titian, Lotto, Vecchio,
Tintoretto ; Titian, Titian—or, as the labels pedantic-
ally insist, Tiziano Vecelli, which certainly sounds
richer. Somehow the acreage of burning chromaticism cloys the senses. One has a feeling that to most
of the Habsburgs the paintings must have been all
one so long as the mixture was *rich*. Yet, examined
individually, and with a fair mind, we find that
these Titians offer a perfect representation of that
painter's astonishing range, in duplicate, in triplicate
—from the " Ecce Homo " to the " Danae," from
"Isabella d'Este" to the Madonnas. They must have

been chosen with care. One cannot really complain. Yet, faced with this lush, sub-tropical exuberance (set off by Correggio's plummy blues and greys), one wishes that the Austrian Habsburgs had loved, say Velasquez, as deeply as Madrid, in the person of the Emperor Charles, loved Titian. Admittedly there are as many Velasquezs here as anywhere outside the Prado, but then, that master was family property, and one feels that with a little trouble more of his work could have been diverted to Vienna. The evidence suggests that the German Habsburgs regarded him highly as a painter of portraits, preferring the Venetians when it came to anything else. Some of his loveliest canvasses are there, pink and blue Infantas and Infantes, to cool the eye, to clear the senses, to freshen with exquisitely painted lacework the perception after the bold Venetian orgies ; but there is, alas, all too little of that Velasquez whom Manet, two centuries after him, spent a lifetime trying not to imitate.

Whether the lacking balance between this and that was due to Imperial preference or not it is impossible to say ; but it is hard not to think that the Venetian splendours were what the Habsburgs, most of them, really called painting. Rudolf seems to have been a genuine connoisseur ; he founded at Prague, which city beneath his reign enjoyed its golden age, a Kunst-und-Wunder-Kammer (a Chamber of Arts and Wonders) notable for its Dürers, Brueghels and Correggios ; but after him the collector's zeal seems to have been vested mainly in the junior members of the family. His successors,

Matthew and Ferdinand II, must have been too
occupied counter-reforming to allow of any great
indulgence in the graces ; but, as the cadets of
English families of substance were so often handed
over to the Church, so the junior Habsburg archdukes, sent from Vienna to govern provinces, seem
to have regarded as their special charge the arts.
At any rate, the Vienna collection of today owes its
present magnificence very much to two of them—
to Leopold William, son of the impossible Ferdinand,
who as Statholder of the Netherlands during
Rembrandt's last years gathered the bulk of the
paintings together, and to the Archduke Ferdinand
of Tyrol. Ferdinand is an interesting figure ; he
created as well as admired, and in Prague today,
on the White Mountain just outside the city, where
the Catholic emperor smashed the Bohemian protestant pretensions, stands the Hvezda Castle, a star-
shaped château in renaissance style, which was
planned by the only Habsburg architect of skill.
Certainly the man seems to have had an eye for
quality, for without his intervention the Vienna
gallery would have had no worthy Raphael—the
presence of the " Madonna al Verde " being attributed to him ; and unquestionably from him comes
what is one of the rarest treasures of the town, if
far from the greatest intrinsically : that is the marvellous and celebrated salt-cellar of Cellini, the only
authenticated instance of his goldsmith's work surviving, made, as his story ramblingly relates, for
the King of France, whose displeasure he was shortly
to earn, and presented by that king to our archduke

of Tyrol. One feels that he must have had a more
fastidious eye than the average member of his
family.

It is difficult to say : the Venetian splendours may
have been what the Habsburgs really called painting.
On the other hand their preponderance may be due
solely to a policy of *laissez-faire*, Venice being easily
accessible. For side by side with Northern Italy we
have the Netherlands, even more accessible and
completely controlled by Habsburg, and although
the collection of Dutch and Flemish paintings is
huge there is about it something of the rag-bag—
a host of minor works, an equal host of major ones,
some astonishing omissions, at least one miracle.
The miracle is " Velvet " Brueghel.

Precisely how these bright, plebeian masterpieces appeared to our exalted family it would be
interesting to know. Most of them seem to have been
originally in the Kunst-und-Wunder-Kammer of
Rudolf at Prague ; but the painter and his son
must have been in favour in high places, for there
is an excellent example of the work of each in the
Liechtenstein collection in the palace just outside the
Inner City. The fact that half the elder Brueghel's
total output is now to be found in this relatively
southern city cannot be an accident. Perhaps it was
simply that Brueghel, like Titian, was handy. Perhaps the freshness of his colour and the humanity
of his ideas were an antidote to Venice. Perhaps
there was simply a craze for him, analogous to 19th-
century slumming ; there are some of these Spanish
Catholics whom one can't see unbending to " The

Rustic Wedding ". Perhaps. . . . But one can never
tell—perhaps the collecting Austrian Habsburgs,
the haunted and impotent Rudolf, really liked these
simple subjects, escaping with delight from the
formidable *grandezza* of the canons of grandfather
Charles. The fact remains that here in this building
is a collection of Brueghels which needs only the
"Adam and Eve in Paradise" from Amsterdam to
perfect its range ; and with these the younger,
" Hellfire ", Brueghel's lovely and most unhellish
" Winter Landscape " with its small black figures
skating on the icy flats.

These alone are enough to make the journey
worth the fare, and, of course, there are other
masterpieces, dozens of them : Van Dycks, Rubens,
Rembrandts, Ruisdael's magnificent " In the Great
Forest ". There is also a treasured Van Eyck, the
" Cardinal of Santa Croce ". Yet considering the
opportunities the omissions are no less striking.
There is no Vermeer in the Imperial collections, yet
the Czernins managed to secure one, that perfect
interior, " The Artist in his Studio " ; nor is there
any Franz Hals to equal the " Willem van Heyt-
hausen " in the Liechtenstein collection housed in
the superb baroque palace which makes this gallery
the most beautiful in Europe. To this collection
indeed, and to the lesser collections of other princes
of the 18th century which are such a glorious feature
of Vienna, or to the Academy of Fine Arts, one is
sooner or later driven. Botticelli, Canaletto, El Greco,
della Robbia and half a dozen other masters are all
best represented in the private galleries—and so is

almost every painter of France whom one can name.
Habsburg, it will be remembered, was " the eternal"
counterpoise to France, and collection suffers for it.

We are not quarrelling with the Vienna gallery.
On the contrary. It includes as many fine things as
any other, only rather curiously chosen. And even
that lack of reasonable balance is of extraordinary
interest. It reminds us that the legendary patrons
of a vanished age were almost as naïve and greedy
as our tradesmen monarchs of today.

There was something in between, however.
After the 16th-century Habsburgs and before the
millionaires there came a finer age ; it has already
been suggested by the paintings in the private
galleries belonging to princes not of the Habsburg
blood. The House of Austria at this point had become
an established institution, had settled down and
ceased collecting pictures, leaving that occupation
to its nobles. In 1657, with the death of Ferdinand
III, who had tided Vienna over the period of exhaustion which followed the Thirty Years' War, the
Hofburg ceased to be the undisputed symbol. It was
to grow a great deal more and remain the Imperial
residence until the end, but although it remained
the ultimate power it was no longer the absolute
centre ; new forces were working fast. Something
was happening to the native Viennese. To all appearances the German artistic consciousness had been
routed entirely by the soft Italian element imported
by the rulers, but now, less than a century after
Solari's Italian cathedral in pink and white marble

at Salzburg, we find neither Italy not Germany triumphant, but something quite new, born of the tension between the alien and native strains: Austria. The note of this new country is the note of Vienna today.

V. THE BELVEDERE

FOR a long time the state of affairs for native
craftsmen had been thoroughly unpropitious.
Austria, when all was said, was German ; its in-
stincts were German, though softened by the
southern aspect and twisted subtly by Slavonic
blood. We have seen how at first the native talent
was wholly Teutonic in expression. We have glanced
at the era of the Stefansdom, when German gothic
was also the symbol of Vienna ; and we have seen
how under Maximilian I German artists and craftsmen were encouraged and Cranach, not Bellini,
was the leader and inspirer, and, later, Dürer the
Imperial pensioner. Then all that was changed.
The Habsburgs, like all new potentates, wanted the
exotic. Italians were imported in increasing numbers. The complaint of the contemporary Viennese
artist or craftsman was the complaint of the contemporary English musician today ; the foreigner
can do no wrong ! It must have been very trying ;
the people had a tradition, and that tradition was
being ignored or trampled down. The successors to
the sculptors of Maximilian's tomb were out of work;
they could not adapt themselves, even if they wanted
to, and even if they could there was little hope for
anyone without a foreign name. At the beginning

of the 17th century the Italian cultural hegemony was undisputed, but still it was a manner imposed from without.

Then, on March 3rd, 1656, at Graz in Lower Austria, there was born a child, the eldest and most important of several who were, all over Austria, to come into the world soon after him, imbued with a new and native spirit in consonance with the age. He was baptised Johann Bernard Fischer von Erlach. That name was to become a symbol of a new age, an age of glory which would persist, lingering on, for nearly two hundred years.

Determined to make a name as an architect, Fischer von Erlach was not dismayed by the sight of Austrian building in Italian hands ; on the contrary. As the child of a new and confident age he was interested in new buildings, not in ruins. The ruins were German, the new buildings Italian ; it was manifest that the best ideas were Italian. It was not enough, however, to learn from the Italians in Vienna, numerous and gifted as these were ; at the age of twenty-four von Erlach set out for Italy itself, North Italy and Rome. He did well to do so, for the great building phase in Italy was drawing to a close, and the Italians in Vienna were cut off from their own tradition. In the winter of 1680, von Erlach's first year in Italy, occurred the death of Giovanni Lorenzo Bernini, at the age of eighty-two. That, if you like, was symbolical. Bernini, architect of the Colonnade of St. Peter's, not seriously troubled by any rivals, had for a long time laid down the law. Now he was dead. Bernini had done most things, but always he retained a formalism, and this formalism was at odds with a new spirit in the air. He had created a baroque, but it sprang more from the mind than the impulse. Lesser rivals, whom he had overshadowed, were otherwise preoccupied; they were filled with a passion for the *expressive* form. Their search was not always happy; but the most important of them, Borromini, probably meant more to von Erlach than all the solemnities of the panjandrum of the age.

The young Austrian saw and drew. Like Goethe in a later century he had come, as must every Northerner, to the land where the orange-trees bloom. Like Goethe he was transported by what he saw. Unlike Goethe, who adorned a dying age, he saw not the sad ruins of a classical antiquity but the vaulting assurance of a modern movement fixed in shining, brand-new elevations. He saw and drew. By way of exercise he seems to have copied existing elevations, then elaborated them, improvising freely, as a master of composition will take an existing theme and draw from it a chain of variations. A better training for the free, spontaneous fancy of the art he was to practise it would be impossible to imagine. For five years he did this, then he went home. For a time, to complete his training, he worked as a decorative painter. In 1687 he was appointed Kaiserliche Hofingenieur. In the same year he was charged with the erection of what is still the most remarkable monument in Vienna, the Trinity Column in the Graben, a pillar raised by order of the Emperor Leopold I as a votive offering of thanksgiving for delivery from the great plague, which smote Vienna some years after it had ravaged London. The original design was not by von Erlach, but by an Italian, Burnacini; in this kind of work, however, with its absolute freedom from architectural form, as much depends on the man in charge of the building as on the designer. Nothing, one feels, can have been nearer the young architect's heart than this free fantasia in stone ; here, at the very beginning of his career, was a final cleavage with Bernini, the panjandrum, an acknowledgement of Borromini's passionate manipulation of stubborn material to express a mental vision. He worked on it and won fame. He had arrived, and at the most propitious moment in the world.

For while he had still been studying in Italy the encroaching Turk had once more pushed up to the very walls of the Inner City, had laid waste the outer suburbs, had been held by Starhemberg and finally pushed back by Sobieski. Vienna had suffered cruelly ; now the reaction came. Whether the Viennese knew that the Turk was done for, once and for all, it is impossible to say ; though, in those days, the defeat of an army of two hundred thousand men must have seemed a pretty final statement of accounts. But whether they knew it or not, they behaved as though all perils were at an end. There was an uprush of vitality; the fortress city, so recently beleaguered, rapidly became a social centre of the highest order, with all the concomitants thereof. The nobility took to building themselves new palaces ; inside the city at first, in curious positions, then, when the walls were at last knocked down, the mediaeval walls built with the Lionheart's ransom money, outside in the open, enclosed by private parks. And, ready to hand, was Fischer von Erlach, the brilliant young architect, supremely gifted to make a Vienna for the Viennese, a new conception. Commission after commission came to him, and soon to another young man, several years his junior, Lukas von Hildebrandt, who was to work with him sometimes in rivalry, sometimes in collaboration. Between them these two (and others following in their footsteps ; for this was a nation-wide renaissance) changed in fifty years the whole face of Vienna, leaving it as we know it today with its peculiar atmosphere which we are trying to suggest.

Until a very few years ago baroque was commonly regarded in this country as a vulgar and trivial excrescence on the architectural corpus. Times have changed. It is understood that at the moment (or it may have been last year) baroque is even fashionable. Be that as it may, and if it is it will not be for long, there is at last in serious people a serious desire to appreciate the mode for what it is, whether they personally can stomach it or not ; and then, looked at closely, sympathetically and from an appropriate point of view, there is seen to be less to stomach than the first astonished glance reported. This change of heart owes itself in the main to Mr. Sacheverell Sitwell and particularly to his two books *Southern Baroque Art* and *German*

Baroque Art. With the first of these Mr. Sitwell was
solitary in an attack on an ancient prejudice ; then,
almost at the same time, appeared Mr. H. V. Lanchester's matter-of-fact, admirable but all too short
monograph on von Erlach himself, this coincidence
suggesting a stirring in the air.

Deeply grateful as we must be, if baroque
appeals to us, to Mr. Sitwell, it is yet possible to
regret his point of view, which emphasises the pretti-
ness of the mode, hiding its greatness. The clue
is the failure to differentiate definitely between
baroque and rococo—" those two excessive and inter-
flowing shadows of the classical merge themselves
into an inseparable whole where there is hardly
anything save a criterion of scale to distinguish
between them ". They interflow, they merge together ; it may be impossible to indicate the line
of fusion ; but the difference between rococo and
the high summer of baroque though certainly one
of scale is also one of spirit, as we shall see, I hope,
before our tour is over.

The stranger in Vienna strolling on his first
day down the Graben, which he will, since that
street is the centre of the city, is taken aback by a
fantastic monument stuck up in the middle of that
short, broad carriage-way which is more like a *place*
than a street. It consists at first sight of a pedestal
with reliefs, and over this an absurd confection in
rather dingy marble of billowing clouds supporting
cherubs and surmounted by the symbolic representation of the Son, the Father and the Holy
Ghost, the gilded sun-rays glittering in the sunlight.

He gives a shrug of amused incomprehension and passes on. We have already passed it by, being more concerned with the Stefansdom, in whose shadow almost it stands. We took it in at a glance as part of the general impression, as contributing to the curious flavour resulting from the contrast between gothic and baroque. Most strangers in Vienna never look any closer, unless with the air of a visitor to a zoo. But this, for us, is an important monument; it celebrates the first appearance of Fischer von Erlach in the streets of the city he was to transfigure. It is also an excellent introduction to baroque ; a better one could not be found.

That is not to say that this Column of the Holy Trinity, or Plague Column, as it is usually called, is a supreme masterpiece of baroque ; there is too much of the *tour de force* about it for absolute satisfaction : but it does display, with extreme purity and straightforwardness, the true nature of the deep impulse behind the greatest baroque. There are no complicating factors. Burnacini, who designed it, was free to follow his fancy wherever it led ; he was not faced with the problem of adapting his imagination to any utilitarian ends, such as the provision of habitable rooms, as in a palace. The only obstacle in the way of perfect realisation of his ideas was the law of gravity, which tied him to the ground. Thus these ideas are found here expressed more completely and logically than in any church or palace ; yet, without a proper appreciation of them, no baroque building can be seen for what it is.

The great barrier between most people and

baroque is founded on an elementary misconception, on the belief that all the apparent fal-lals are in fact intended as fal-lals, or imposed ornamentation. A simple building is imagined, and to this simple fabric every device of fancy is *attached*, like 19th-century gimcrack. Nothing could be further from the truth, and a moment's open-minded contemplation of this column should give one an inkling of the truth; for here, where utilitarian considerations do not enter the picture, the " ornamentation " is no less than the whole, and the whole is the " ornamentation ". This is not a simple column plastered with cherubs and clouds; it is, in obvious intention, a great block of stone transfigured. And that brings us to the baroque idea, the baroque of Austria—of Fischer von Erlach, Lukas von Hildebrandt, Brandauer and many others.

The idea is a perfect and logically to be expected expression of the 18th-century genius, or megalomania: the imposition by man of his own order on rude nature. That, of course, pushed to its proper end, is a wildly romantic conception, as romantic as anything dreamt of by Novalis, and it *was* pushed to its end. That end, in the instance of architecture, was the subjugation of all materials to the architect's purpose. *All* materials.

Hitherto the architects of Europe had respected their materials. They had used stone, wood, metal, and in their designs they had taken into account the qualities and attributes of these things, planning their elevations in sympathy with these qualities. The stone and wood, in place as blocks of stone and

beams of wood, had then been carved with an eye
to decoration, but the rights of stone to be stone
and the rights of wood to be wood were usually
respected. That is an approach so closely in line with
that of the most articulate of our own contemporary
architects and sculptors, whose respect for the
materials they work in is so extreme that to some
they may appear more in the manner of fetish-
worshippers than proper sculptors with wills of
their own, that one cannot feel that the present
interest in baroque is more than a passing fashion;
for anything in more direct opposition to the most
vaunted work of today it would be impossible to
imagine. In the Graben column the only thing in the
world that matters to the designer is the designer's
conception of heaven and earth and the universe;
everything else, in this instance the marble, is employed as a vulgar means to the sublimest of ends.
The stone is tortured, spurned and put in its proper
place, a slave to the master's purpose. If the
stone is pretty in itself, if, for instance, it will take
a high polish or has a natural coloration, well and
good; these facts are noted with pleasure by the
architect, who proceeds to take advantage of them—
but they are of interest to him only in so far as
they can be of service to his own preconceived ends;
never in any other way. The humane notion pre-
valent here and there today that the sculptor's task
is to help the stone to find its own fullest self-
expression was infinitely remote from these 17th-
century artificers as they sought out the loveliest
shades in marble from the quarries of Carrara. They

L

and their contemporaries were putting nature in its
place; the Alps, which they had to cross to reach
Italy, and with which nothing could be done, were
an abomination and a nuisance.

The architects of the Viennese baroque, Fischer
von Erlach, that is to say, Lukas von Hildebrandt,
and others, were, in effect, glorified sculptors and
decorators. It is possible that the germ of their idea
came from painting, in particular from Michelangelo's ceiling paintings in the Sistine Chapel;
here for the first time, as Mr. Lanchester has pointed
out, decoration and architecture are one and in-
divisible: the painting is not *applied* to a bare and
inviting surface, but is an organic part of the whole
conception of the roof. It seems to me, too, that the
stone-carving of the later gothic masters, such as
Anton Pilgram of Brunn, whose pulpit in the
Stefansdom at Vienna we have already admired,
may have struck the new architects with a new and
special force. The elaborate openwork carving of
Pilgram belongs to the decadence of gothic, and the
spirit behind it is not the spirit behind the carving
of the Graben column; Pilgram, that is to say, is
not using stone as a malleable material suitable for
the expression of a private vision; on the contrary,
he is engaged in a *tour de force*, pitting himself
against the stone to show what a determined mind
can do to it. But it seems to me that somewhere at
the back of his mind there may have been a vague
idea that all materials, including stone, were there
to be used as the designer chose to use them, irre-
spective of their innate qualities; and after the

Pilgram pulpit of the early 16th century the appearance of the Graben column towards the end of the 17th seems not astonishing.

But Michelangelo was the vital influence; in the light of his achievements the next step, plainly, is to eliminate entirely the principle of applied decoration by using paint and gilding impartially with stone and wood, metalwork and stucco, as part of the fabric itself. The architect desired an effect, he wished to express some private vision of his own, and the painter, the carver, the gilder, the plasterer, were so many craftsmen to be directed by him that their output might be employed in the realisation of this vision, subservient to it. The apotheosis of this principle we may see embodied in the most perfect of all baroque interiors, the Court Library in the Hofburg. Here we may see how a great architect working in close co-operation with a gifted painter and with other craftsmen of high talent may perfectly realise the baroque ideal, the fusion together and the blending of all materials into a whole almost recklessly conceived. The painter was Daniel Gran, who also painted the ceilings of the Schwarzenberg Palace, perhaps the most gifted of the Austrian painters who succeeded, sometime after the architects came into power, the all-powerful Italians— Antonio Burnacini, Domenico Martinelli, and Fratel Pozzo, who was brought from Italy by a Liechtenstein, and whose finest work is in the frescoes of the glorious Liechtenstein palace.

Gran has in this library subdued himself entirely (as the painter does in every successful room of the period) to the vision of the architect, and, in return, the architect has provided an incomparable and immortal (the word is relative) setting for his art. In this astonishing hall, which is the high-water mark of baroque interior decoration (the age of rococo was to follow very soon), it is, at the first quick, comprehensive glance, impossible to tell where one material begins and another ends, where wood gives place to metal, where stone supports them both, where carving merges into painting. That is the dream of baroque made substance: the flowing, never-interrupted line, pursued now through one medium, now through another, and expressing as intimately as though moulded by the hand in some malleable material the original design—a design, in the master's mind, existing as a vision, not as a design in wood, or stone, or metal, but as design in the absolute, here triumphantly carried out in whatever blending of materials could best be bent to the realisation of the dream, and by a group of devoted craftsmen prepared to sink their individualities in the whole, knowing that through the whole their work would live. That is baroque.

The mode plainly depended for its fulfilment absolutely on the existence of large numbers of talented artists and craftsmen, from the mural painter to the stone-mason, who, while being men of responsibility, creativeness and initiative, were yet prepared to work in close collaboration with the chief designer, the architect. We see this essential *seriousness* in the life of Fischer von Erlach himself,

The Karlskirche

The Library in the Hofburg

who, before setting up as an architect on his own, worked (and not because he had to) as a mural painter.

This condition unfulfilled there could have been no baroque, just as there could be no symphonies or operas without the provision of large numbers of sensitive musicians ready to work in collaboration with and finally subject to a leader or conductor. In architecture that state of affairs has not lasted, hence its atrophy; for although the mode of baroque with its air of spontaneous improvisation and its perpetual wrestling with the law of gravity stood in especial need of gifted and resourceful men to execute the plans of the designer, all other vital architectural phases have depended, to a more or less degree, on the fulfilment of the same condition. Nor is this so elysian a state of affairs as a first glance might suggest. There was, I take it, a certain *esprit de corps*, but also one may be sure that there was little in the way of self-conscious heroics; the man of great talents nobly sacrificing his individuality to the man of genius for the common good—that sort of thing. I imagine the circumstances were taken very much for granted: a man could paint, and painting was used in buildings, and quite obviously he couldn't be allowed to paint what he liked, how he liked and where he liked without reference to the sentiments of the builder. That state of affairs, when all is said, is in music still seen today in humdrum action. The proud prima donna and the first violin do not quarrel with the pre-eminence of Toscanini; on the contrary: in him they find the means of getting their daily bread and practising their art.

This, heaven forbid, is not an oblique attack on individualism, an appeal to the workers of the world to unite. To suppress, self-consciously, the individualistic impulse in us today is to frustrate our natures. With his usual penetration Jakob Burckhardt called the Renaissance the discovery of the individual. The Renaissance was the birth of an age of which we form the tail; a tail cannot be asked to change its spots. The individual is already discovered in Fischer von Erlach's day ; he himself is a notable specimen of the genus; but discovery does not imply glorification, and it was left to the decline of the age to exalt its individuals to impossible heights. Von Erlach was famous in his day, but his fame was not at odds with the community of purpose finding expression in collaboration with him. Von Erlach was a figure of the Renaissance—the Austrian Renaissance, which came late, which is included in and comprehended by the general Renaissance of Europe, using the term now technically—but the upward rush of vitality which bore him aloft was simply the pent-up energy of a local community suddenly finding its way. This lost community of purpose (it has lingered in music a little, for obvious reasons) was a blissful state of affairs, but it *is* lost, and crying over spilt milk is unprofitable. It was lost with the beginning of the decadence, naturally, inevitably and with many glorious consequences, including the whole of the artistic activity from 1763 onwards. (Hermann Bahr gives the date of the loss of Silesia to Prussia as the start of Austrian decadence, and that date is as good as any.) It will return only with the birth of a new culture, whatever form that may take; but an attempt to restore it artificially by means of polysyllabic manifestos is a waste of time. It simply will not go with decline, and if we believe that the new age begins with us we are flattering ourselves. The old one is not dead yet; we have still some way to go; and it would be pleasant if we could bring ourselves to go that way as gracefully as possible, not making ourselves ridiculous by leaping into the air and slapping our chests and uttering loud cries of welcome to the setting sun. That sort of mistake was permissible in the '90's; today it is merely silly.

To return to the architects of late 17th-century Vienna, to Fischer von Erlach. No such thoughts troubled their minds. They went ahead, following their leader, who took work where it came, finding an ever surer touch, elaborating freely and with the versatility of genius in a mode which won the approval of his fellow citizens, who deemed his fantasies to express things very perfectly. He built palaces, churches and monuments, and all these stand today. In them may be found beauty and marvellous skill and opportunism.

To mention here by name all the engaging monuments left by von Erlach, Hildebrandt and others would be too tedious. There is no end to them and Baedeker has all that matter. But some few are of striking interest and cannot be ignored ; perhaps these will throw their light on the unmentioned rest.

We have dwelt lightly on the column in the
Graben, that curvilinear pyramid of cumulus in
petrifaction surmounted by the emblems of the
Catholic faith and adorned by the kneeling figure
of the Catholic Emperor. This, we have seen, is
baroque made absolute, untrammelled by utilitarian
ends. We shall not see its like again in Vienna,
although in other towns of Austria, notably in Linz,
there are things resembling it. Plainly, our baroque
architects, however enamoured of plastic massing,
the flowing line, the sculpturesque composition (to
use the words of Mr. Lanchester), could not spend
their days composing memorials to plagues entirely
out of clouds, those pearly ephemera which lend
themselves so perfectly to the expression of the
above idea as applied to Carrara stone. To pay for
monuments there had to be princes, or prelates ;
and these required palaces or churches for themselves. Fischer von Erlach and his colleagues built
both ; one of the first buildings executed entirely
to his own design was a new palace (or the greater
part of it) for Prince Eugene of Savoy. This is in as
sharp a contrast to the Burnacini column as could
be found. It is built in a narrow side-street, the
Himmelpfortgasse, leading from the Kärntnerstrasse ; and today, as the Ministry of Finance, it is
one of those unexpected palaces which we have
already noticed, standing cheek by jowl with
cavernous tenements exuding the odour of *gulasch*.
It is baroque adapted to mediaeval conditions, for,
unlike so many of von Erlach's works, it is built in
the heart of a city which was still encircled by

mediaeval walls. It reminds us forcibly that its creator was an accomplished architect, knowing all the rules, as well as a creature of fantasy; and anyone who thinks of these men of the baroque as showmen, mountebanks, exhibitionists who were lost without a large space of ground and no topographical obligations, has only to look at this palace to see that he is wrong. The Himmelpfortgasse is an extremely narrow street, as befits its name, which means the Gates of Heaven, and Prince Eugene, who decided to build himself a house there, was an extremely important personage. Von Erlach, without spoiling the line of the street, has given him all the pomp he could desire. The problem which he set himself was to devise an elevation which impressed when seen obliquely, for there is no room to admire it from the front; and this he has achieved magnificently by emphasising the lateral thrust as against the vertical. The whole thing is a perfect example of adaptation to environment and a monumental proof of the essential stability of the period and its chief artisans.

Once, it seems to me, one has acknowledged the purpose behind the Graben column and the honesty of the palace in the Himmelpfortgasse, the other palaces and churches may be regarded with a clearer eye. On another page there will be found a photograph of the Karlskirche, another memorial to plague, another triumph of baroque, regarded by many as von Erlach's masterpiece. This, once upon a time, stood in green fields without the city walls. It must have appeared as a symbol of the new conception,

splendid, alone, and free as air. Now, lying just
beyond the Parkring, the space around it is constricted and the neighbouring buildings of the 19th
century form a poor setting for the gem. When he
designed this masterpiece—and it is plainly conceived and planned as one ; any old print showing
its original setting proves that—von Erlach doubtless
knew that one day the fields would be built upon,
but he doubtless expected too that some considera-
tion would be paid his own conception. He, with
his lifelong preoccupation with the new, his
absolute freedom from the clutches of past ages,
achieved as few have done " that true harmony of
which modern art is afraid, for it never realises that
the new always enhances the old ". But the buildings which sprang up round the Karlskirche when
von Erlach was dead are not new ; they do not enhance the old, and all harmony is absent. That
makes it more difficult to appreciate the old.

Even then there is still sufficient space around
it for the church to be seen whole. Unlike St. Paul's,
which has to be viewed piecemeal, which is never
really *seen*, it stands up from the ground a building,
not a mysterious, soaring dome. And if for the present writer the Minoritenkirche is the most cherished
silhouette of the whole city because it stands for a
quality of sternness which Vienna has lost to her
undoing, the bright green dome, the exquisitely
proportioned clock towers, the bold twin Trajan's
pillars of the Church of St. Charles Borromeo is
the incomparable symbol of Vienna as it is, or almost
is: the Vienna of the princely palaces, the palaces

of the Liechtensteins, the Kinskys, the Schönborns, the Harrachs, the Czernins, the Lobkowitzes and the Schwarzenbergs ; the Vienna of Schönbrunn and the lovelier parts of the Hofburg ; the Vienna of the Spanish Riding School ; the Vienna of Haydn ; the Vienna transcendentalised by Mozart, or perfumed and embalmed by Hofmannsthal and Richard Strauss ; the proud Vienna of the blazing altars, side-chapels and canopies *ad Dei gloriam* ; the Vienna of the 18th century which, at the height of its glory, went soft, and remained soft ; the Vienna which achieved an elegance, a refinement, a poise, which seemed the justification of our Western contribution, the city culture—and which, as a result, is ever denied an understanding of its greatest men —Mozart and Schubert, who were yet produced by it.

The whole association of Vienna with baroque is curious. The age of baroque, which was also the age of Gluck in music, was for that city the summit of its renaissance ; the decadence was yet to come ; and yet, so far as architecture went, its renaissance was expressed in a decadent style. It cannot be argued otherwise, I think, than that the Italians inspiring von Erlach and his colleagues were, as far as Italy was concerned, architects of a decadence. The seeds of decadence were in Michelangelo, who was his own law, and in the architecture of Bernini the purity of the original impulse which was the Renaissance has lost its transparency and become stained with many subtleties. It is impossible to see Italian baroque, no matter how much we may value it, as anything other than an expression of decadence. The signs of decline are all there, signs which will be apparent later when we come to the decadence of Austria. . . . Yet, as we were about to say, in Vienna, on the northern slopes of the Alps which shelter Italy, this same style of art which in Italy is decadent is employed as an expression of rebirth. There is something ominous in that, boding no good for the future. The situation which it suggests is artificial and exotic. Something is left out.

That something is slow growth. Sleeping for too long after the close of the Middle Ages (and we already know the reason for that spiritual and intellectual drowsiness), possessing little creative will of its own, our city suddenly awakens and starts afresh, not from the beginning but from the dubious height which it had taken the Italians three centuries of furious activity to reach.

An analogy seems to exist between 18th-century Vienna and 20th-century New York: in the one the sudden maturity was coloured by the mind, in the other by the instinct of acquisitiveness ; but both were induced from outside ; neither was the inevitable, healthy outcome of slow maturing. Both may be seen as the florescence of exotic cuttings arbitrarily grafted to an uncultured stock. Both lack the faithfulness to type, the robust habit of the plant slowly raised from the seed. Therein lies Vienna's tragedy; but also her supreme, exotic beauty and the blessed lateness of her flowering.

There was no thought of doom in the head of

von Erlach as he drew up the plans for his astonishing church to St. Charles Borromeo, nor were he or any of his colleagues and assistants the playthings of decline. Bernini and Borromini in Italy had been elaborating fanciful variations on an old idea, but the products of their fantasy came to Austria as a new idea, stimulating and suggestive. The curious imitations of Trajan's column flanking the dome of the Karlskirche were not put there by von Erlach through the wanton ingenuity of indolence. They were, in his mind (and remain today if we remember the purpose of baroque as revealed in the Graben column and credit its chief creator with architectural sense, as we must in view of the Prince Eugene palace), powerfully expressive, devised by him to enhance the massive majesty of the dome. Take, in imagination, those columns away and that design is seen to be incomplete, indicating that the columns were not an idle, irresponsible afterthought but as much a part of the original conception as the minarets of an oriental mosque. As for the main fabric itself, there is no denying the splendour of the conception : indeed, so evident is this that, doubting the solidity of anything so immediately effective, the temptation is to ignore the detail; but one has only to glance at the photograph to realise the mastery of the man who could, as a fundament for bewildering elaboration, achieve the exquisite proportions of the twin belfry towers, one of which is shown. This is the kind of thing which should be remembered when much is made of the falseness of baroque—the sham and the emptiness, the imposing façades owing balance and rhythm not to the fulfilment of structural requirements but to the architect's whim ; the windows which admit no light, the doorways leading nowhere.

That may indicate, in fact it does, a decadence of architecture, but not, in von Erlach, a decadence of spirit. For in his mind the façade was everything, the *appearance*, that is, both within and without. This is something other than the spirit which would cover a steel skeleton with Tudor beams; that is no more than an admission of impotence, the necessity to imitate something that has gone and the determination to use the most convenient means to hand. The lightless windows of baroque are not meaningless at all. Architecturally they may have no justification, but the baroque designers of Vienna were not, as we have already insisted, architects as normally understood ; they were a new species, sculptors, architects and interior decorators in one. They were not ruled by the determination to make of a necessary building as fine a harmony as possible; they used the building as a pretext for a necessary design. But also they had sufficient architectural sense of the traditional kind to adapt their fantasy with astonishing success to the utilitarian purpose of the building. They merely held themselves free to follow their star provided the *purpose* of the building (as conceived by its proprietor) was not thereby frustrated.

The difference is the difference between a room deprived of a window for the sake of exterior symmetry and a room provided with a superfluous window to that same end.

We have seen enough now of Fischer von Erlach to have some conception of his range. The few works we have glanced at with some attention display his genius in its various aspects and at the same time illustrate sufficiently the meaning of baroque. To review the whole of this man's output would be a very long job ; in a book of this nature it would resolve itself into a catalogue of palaces, temporal and spiritual—and also we should have to go outside Vienna. We have dwelt at length on von Erlach, saying little or nothing of Hildebrandt and his other, lesser colleagues. This, æsthetically speaking, is not just to Hildebrandt, who created masterpieces as fine as anything of von Erlach's; but historically there is no choice. Fischer von Erlach started first ; his too was very much the larger output; it was he who changed the face of Vienna, with Hildebrandt as aider and abettor. There were others, too, lacking famous names. For beautiful building went on in Vienna long after von Erlach's death in the early 18th century. It diminished into rococo, but there were still, much later, signs that the original spirit was not dead. As an illustration of the extraordinary *saturation* of Austria by this mode we may return to the Peterskirche, off the Graben, which we have already glimpsed. We see there the main portico in grey marble, evidently all part of von Erlach's original conception; but it was not. It was added long after the architect's death, and in its perfect sympathy with the fabric of the building is eloquent of the naturalness of the mode. The fact that the designer of the porch was an Italian, Andrea Altomonte, is neither here nor there.

The masterpiece of Lukas von Hildebrandt is the Belvedere Palace, which stands on a hill beyond the Karlskirche and well outside the Inner City. That was one of the buildings made possible by the bursting of the walls, and never has an architect made finer use of space. There is no doubt that here is the loveliest palace in all Vienna, infinitely palatial yet infinitely graceful. There is no doubt, either, that von Erlach could have rivalled it—although with his eye for masses he would never have achieved the fairy lightness of Hildebrandt, whose genius for combining the imposing with the unpompous is here beautifully displayed. But it was Hildebrandt who had the opportunity—the chance to build imperially on what was virgin ground. Von Erlach, as senior architect, had much to do with the rebuilding and extension of the Hofburg, but here was limited by all kinds of considerations; he built many palaces for princes, but it needs a royalty to commission a Belvedere palace ; and although he was given the greatest opportunity of all, the designing of the new summer palace at Schönbrunn, the Habsburgs being jealous of Versailles, the building was put off and his plans were never realised— the present building being done to Maria Theresa's order by an Italian called Pacassi, who was well on the downward path. Thus the masterpiece of Hildebrandt remains, in Vienna, also the baroque master-

piece of the palace style, as distinct from what might
be called the inflated mansion style.

It was built as a summer palace by Prince Eugene
of Savoy, whose winter palace in the Himmelpfortgasse we have already seen ; but when Prince
Eugene died the Habsburgs stepped in and bought
it ; probably they deemed it too imposing to be the
seat of any subject prince. The Savoys, when all was
said, had to be allowed a certain latitude : they were
an ancient reigning family, entirely independent,
and apt to figure as the saviours of any cause they
cared to stand for ; quite recently Prince Eugene
himself had inflicted severe defeat on the Turks
whom Sobieski had forced to retreat from Vienna ;
he had, very much, the Imperial ear. For any other
prince to live there, even if he could afford to buy
it and keep it up, would have been quite another
matter. Anyway, it is amusing to imagine the
family counsels (if indeed there were any) in the
Hofburg which led to its change of ownership.
Having been bought and thus rendered innocuous
it was used for many years primarily to house the
Habsburg pictures and other objects of art. Later
on Habsburg representatives took to living in the
upper part, and it was from that splendour that
the fatal archduke, Franz Ferdinand, set out with
Sophie Chotek, his wife, to visit Sarajevo and take
command of the manœuvres on the Serbian frontier.
Since then it has stood empty—a monument to those
people, among others, who organise manœuvres on
other people's frontiers.

.   .   .   .   .   .

M

In our contemplation of the glories of pure art we have rather forgotten the Habsburgs. They are still there. Fischer von Erlach himself had to be recognised by the Court before he could become a fashionable architect. His emperors were Leopold I and Joseph I. But although they were still supreme in Austria, and were to remain so for another two centuries, it is not the merest accident that at this period of burgeoning vitality we find ourselves forgetting them. The Belvedere was completed in 1720. Until the end of the 17th century the life of Vienna still centred on the Hofburg, as it had done since the Middle Ages. From the Hofburg came all evil and all good. With the death of Ferdinand III a new phase began; there was a spiritual revolution of the subtlest and gentlest kind imaginable. The symbol of it is none other than the Belvedere itself, but that is to stand another fifty years before any great change is noticeable. Then, looking back, it may be seen as a portent of the decentralisation of cultural and political control, which was bound to occur and increase and which is bound up with the imminent decline. It is a magnificent palace, the shell of princely power and patronage, commanding the Inner City and built by the representative of an alien strain. The rise of these princely families puts a totally different complexion on our city, the complexion by which we know it today. It was they who thenceforward set the cultural pitch, they who advised and quarrelled with, or guided, the sceptred hand. With Ferdinand II we find Habsburg relying for support on soldiers of genius, the Wallensteins and Tillys, employed by and subject to the Crown. The Emperor is no longer capable of personal leadership in the field. With Leopold I we reach a further and deeper striking change : the policy of the Crown, not merely the execution of it, is devised or interfered with and distorted by paid advisers. These quickly gained in power, but they never became supreme. Strong men like Kaunitz were severely curbed ; but weak men like Aerenthal were strong enough to bring the mighty fabric to which they added nothing crashing down. The revolution, of course, was never properly completed. In spite of the rise of a ministerial system Habsburg, unlike Hanover, kept the power of the final word, and exercised this power. Confusion was bound to arise. In the 19th century a foreign minister could read in his morning newspaper that his emperor had, without consulting him, made some decision of extreme importance which was probably a reversal of all considered ministerial policy to date. But although the Crown, according to its humour, could accept or reject the recommendations of its ministers, the ministers were there, pursuing their own policies. Austria could no longer point to the Hofburg saying " that is the unique source of all that happens in this country for good or ill ". This process was surely a revolution. It began with Leopold.

The character of that gentleman himself may have hastened its acceleration. He is sometimes called " the Great ", but it is not easy to see why ; to look at him is not much help. He was, says Coxe, " of a weak and sickly constitution, low in stature, of a saturnine complexion, ordinary in countenance, and distinguished with an unusual portion of the Austrian lip. His gait was stately, slow and deliberate ; his air was pensive, his address awkward, his manner uncouth, his disposition cold and phlegmatic. He was attached to the Spanish dress, customs and etiquette, and usually appeared in a coat of black cloth, ornamented with a large Order of the Golden Fleece, scarlet stockings, and a Spanish hat decorated with a scarlet feather." I do not know if he wore high heels. To appreciate him to the full one has to see him depicted in relief seated in a victorious if precarious attitude upon a prancing charger, crowned with a laurel wreath, greaves of gold upon his legs, golden mail of the Roman pattern sustaining a protuberant belly. This was the man who ushered in the splendour of the Austrian rebirth. Perhaps he was great because his was the honour of expelling the Turk once and for all from Europe ; on the other hand it was his fault, or his ministers', that the Turks got to Vienna at all ; nor did he himself stay to see them off the premises. Retiring in some ignominy to the country, leaving Vienna to its fate, he there learned with embarrassed astonishment that his generals, reinforced by the Polish King, had managed to save it for him. He returned amid perfunctory cheers to find John Sobieski being fêted not only by the people but also by the nobles as their redeemer, but, perhaps owing to his " cold and phlegmatic disposition ", he could not bring himself to invite the saviour to the Hofburg ; instead, clad in his customary black, he rode out to the field of battle and there uttered some stereotyped remarks, like a general conferring a medal on a private.

This Leopold, who had been intended for the Church, who lived like a recluse, and who had been elected Emperor in preference to Louis XIV of France, who, in the War of the Spanish Succession, was to be his deadliest enemy, appears quite unmistakably as the first of the modern Habsburgs. In his Court he set a tone which was to persist until the 20th century—the rigid formalism, the gloomy Spanish airs, the insistence on sixteen quarterings to the coat of arms of any aspirant to Court society— on the other hand the painfully self-conscious attitude towards the very poor, the ease of access accorded the meanest subject—and so on ; all this resulting in an artificial society with the emphasis placed on the extremes, the highly privileged high aristocracy, the feudally pampered lowest orders, with no notice whatsoever taken of what should have been the great middle-class, as everybody knows the backbone of any healthy nation, which in Austria was discouraged almost out of existence. You were either born an aristocrat to rule or a pauper to receive largesse. The bourgeois did not exist—though later there was an extensive class of civil servants. It is all very like Franz Josef ; and Leopold's " cold and phlegmatic disposition ", relieved by a curious and fitful streak of kindness and occasional manifestations of shrewdness (as when this devout Catholic refused to recognise his beloved Jesuits as suitable tutors for a future Emperor), and

the sensitiveness to public opinion which so complicated the acts of a weakish character borne down
with principles—all these live again in the last great
Habsburg of all.

The era of the Hofburg is over. Vienna is no
longer a fortress. The cause of Habsburg aggrandisement is no longer a straightforward issue ; other
factors have arisen, calling for other methods. The
chief of these is the new power of the North German
states of Prussia and Brandenburg resulting from
the Treaty of Westphalia which marked the close
of the Thirty Years' War. Although Leopold, and
his successor Joseph I, and his successor Charles VI
are engaged principally with France over the matter
of the Spanish succession, and although this struggle
is as bitter as can be, the game is becoming too
complicated for the hereditary head of one family,
however ancient, to play entirely on his own. And
already there is something academic about this
Spanish struggle. The Austrian throne lost Spain
and gained the Netherlands, but these were to be
more of an embarrassment than an asset. And if it
had won Spain, what earthly good could it have been
at that time of day? England, France and Austria
no longer had the field of Europe to themselves.
Balances of power had gone beyond the realm of
elementary mathematics. At this very moment
when Vienna approached the peak of her glory two
unexpected figures, a woman and a man, were born,
who, more than any others, were to cause its downfall: Frederick the Great of Prussia, who was born in
1712 in Berlin ; Catherine the Great of Russia, born

a German princess at Stettin in 1729. And although, perhaps in accordance with some secret law, the Habsburg strain at that moment threw up a figure to oppose them of a stature unprecedented for many reigns, Maria Theresa was not a genius and she was only one in face of two; those two, moreover, having everything to gain and nothing to lose and both full of that singleness of purpose met only when young strength discovers itself confined. New wine is poured into the ancient European bottle—with what results !

Spain, which the Habsburgs of the early 18th century so deeply coveted, would not have helped them here. Thus that great War of the Spanish Succession, which gained for British regiments so many of their proudest battle honours—Blenheim, Malplaquet !—cannot but seem a little silly. The grand old men of Europe stand round absorbed in their leisured, immemorial game, oblivious of the bustling crudeness of a new generation so soon to break it up.

All this was not apparent to Leopold. Why should it have been ? Nor to Joseph, nor to Charles VI. But Maria Theresa, who was a great woman and a shrewd and far-seeing one, was oppressed by all manner of misgivings. Her reign is generally regarded as most glorious, and indeed it was. But she herself was a disappointed woman. If she did not realise precisely what was wrong she was shrewd enough and sensitive enough to feel convinced that somewhere something was very wrong indeed. Like England at this very moment she perjured herself

and lost her country's honour in ceaseless efforts
to keep the peace, only (thus far unlike England) to
land herself in wars of a disastrous nature. Filled
with vague forebodings of calamity her whole life
was spent in a sustained endeavour to keep her face
to the peril which was to strike from she knew not
which direction. The devoutest of Catholics, she
yet, for the greater good, suppressed the Jesuits and
forbade her Church to communicate direct with
Rome. Realising that the Roman Empire was now
nothing but a mockery she turned her attention to
the hereditary lands, hoping that judicious education
of the common people might help to weld these
polyglot dominions into a loyal and sympathetic
whole—only to find that the speechless made
articulate turns and rends Pygmalion. She had none
of the crass, material optimism of Joseph II, her son
and successor, who was ready for anything at any
time. Much of her energies were spent restraining
him from shady transactions in foreign affairs. The
whole policy of her time was the fruit of triangular
tension between Joseph her son, Kaunitz her great
minister, and herself, a state of affairs which seemed
to her most dire. Her fears were not merely for the
moral fabric of her heritage but also for its physical
safety. Joseph wanted to pull down the outer ring
of fortifications built when the mediaeval inner walls
had been razed to make room for the flowering of
baroque. His mother would not listen to him. She
was afraid. She feared, or said she feared, the return
of the Turk, whose last appearance she could just
remember. The Turk did not return ; perhaps she

had never expected him ; but the Prussians came, and the French. She had been right about those walls—but what humiliation in that knowledge of rightness ! Seventy years before, while Louis XIV idled in the grounds of his new palace outside the walls of Paris, Leopold had had to flee Vienna, giving it up for lost ; now, when at last all on the surface was well, when Vienna had become the cultural centre of Europe, when she had her own Versailles just completed on the outskirts of the city, when she had control of half the continent of Europe, even then she could not feel secure. It was a curious position.

Vienna has never been secure. That accounts for the brilliance of her culture when it came, and for its shallowness. Nearly a century after the rest of Europe she made her gesture and tore down the walls. She crammed her 17th century into a span of fifty years, most of these coeval with what was the 18th century elsewhere. Her 18th century began when that period was almost done with in other parts of Europe, lingering on well into the 19th ; lingering on, in fact, for ever. For the Vienna of today, in spite of violent change, is still the Vienna of Maria Theresa's day—or a faint reflection of that former splendour. In 1789 occurred the revolution in France. At much the same time in England the Industrial Revolution was beginning. Vienna, at that time, was engaged in the glory of *living*. Her culture had arrived too late to be affected immediately by the universal spirit arising from the weariness of France and England. She was still young.

And when weariness came to her there was no longer in the air the first stirrings of a materialist enthusiasm and faith to give her new (if false) direction. She continued, getting wearier, disillusioned—seeing the straits to which the new spirit was bringing her neighbours, understandably choosing to avoid that evil yet lacking the vitality to find another way, turning thus in on herself, devoting herself to the vain task of preserving her own withering beauty. But even today there is still beauty left, a beauty of the 18th century, backed by the grandeur of the 17th. It begins with the Belvedere, the symbol of our spiritual revolution.

The palace consists of two buildings, one gorgeous and symmetrical, the other utilitarian, a low, cool, rambling affair of stucco ; the Upper and the Lower Belvedere. It is built on the slope of a gentle hillside commanding the Inner City, and Hildebrandt, who planned the palace in relation to its gardens, also laid out by him, broke up this slope into terraces supporting velvet lawns with flowerbeds, tall clipped hedges, ornamental pools, fountains, statuary, espaliers. The baroque designer here, not content with the dead materials of the builder's and sculptor's art, has wrought into his pattern the face of living nature. The centre-piece of the fancy is the Upper Belvedere standing on the hilltop, and the gardens, falling away from the imposing doors, are arranged to display its charm as a jewel in an exquisite setting. Planned in any other age a building of this size could never have escaped a certain ponderousness—ponderousness, in fact, would have

been demanded of it ; but so ingeniously has Hildebrandt disposed his masses, so broken and fluttered
is the sky-line by the dispersal of the great bulk into
three central blocks, flanked first by wings and then
by fanciful pavilions, that nothing lighter could
possibly be imagined. Such is the effect of lightness,
indeed, that a mental effort is required to record its
size. The northern aspect with the gardens descend-
ing from the topmost gravel terrace is, I suppose,
the finest; but the south façade is no less beautiful.
Entering the iron gates from a drab and rather
noisy street, one is transported by the sudden vision
of a fairy palace, ornamented so profusely that the
effect is one of an airy improvisation suddenly
caught and held in stone. And there at one's feet is
an artificial lake, a plain, unislanded expanse,
reaching, it seems, to the very walls of the palace,
which stands there lightly, like an image in a dream,
aloof beyond the mirror-shallow pool.

From the falling gardens the prospect of the city
is extraordinary. One might be, one *is*, physically
in the 18th century. The 20th seems far away ; the
19th does not exist. Odd parts of the town are
glimpsed through clustered trees—the spire of St.
Stephen's against a Canaletto sky and the swelling
hills beyond ; but here one exists in a self-sufficient
world. The spirit is contained by the silence of a
summer's day, scarcely murmurous, a silence of
ancient fruit-trees hoary-barked and trained on
horizontal lines, of glassy ornamental pools faintly
rippled by some dipping fly, a faint murmur of bees,
a gleam of marble statuary, still cool to the touch,

caught between green leaves, a fragrant stillness above the velvet lawns occasionally stirred by the breath of an intermittent breeze, a silence emphasised and displayed against the unreal screaming of high circling swifts ; and looking back, the fine low symmetry of the deserted palace, the roof-top glittering, the blinded windows in the grey front dark in shade. . . . Far on the left the tall dome of the Karlskirche, bright copper green, flashes its gold cross above the hidden city. Bordering these garden walls on either side are other gardens, scarcely less beautiful than ours : the Schwarzenberg park on the left with its palace built by von Erlach and Hildebrandt between them, an oval central bay with wide-flung wings ; on the right the Salesian Nunnery, another baroque masterpiece, standing in lovely grounds with a domed chapel, brightly stuccoed within ; beyond that the botanic gardens, and, away to the front, bordering the 19th-century Ring, and wholly hiding it, the tree-tops of the Stadtpark with its cool and shady lakeside walks.

We stand now at the heart of the old aristocratic quarter, the source and symbol of Vienna's elegance. Even the street which passes at the foot of all these gardens, the Rennweg, seems untouched by modern aims. Now it is the high street of the diplomatic quarter, serving the Embassy mansions which are built in what was once the private park of Metternich ; his palace is now the Italian Embassy. The smaller streets are congeries of lesser mansions. It is a fabulous triangle, contained by the Rennweg with the Metternich park and the Prince Eugenstrasse with the Rothschild park, converging in the Schwarzenbergplatz, its celebrated fountain cooling the air with the atomised spray of a jet which makes a drifting rainbow a hundred feet above the shallow basin.

And now at last we have our Vienna. We have absorbed the old and come to the new; for there is nothing newer than the 18th century—nothing, that is, that counts. Schönbrunn, which followed the Belvedere, and takes us into the period of rococo, the age of Maria Theresa, is as much Vienna now as it was in Mozart's time. It means less now; so does Vienna.

We have defeated the Ringstrasse, which threw itself at our heads as we entered the city, trying forcibly to draw the eye from finer, mellower splendours. We can return to it, when and where we like, and on our own terms. Nevertheless, we shall not do so yet. Over a century lies between the abounding conviction of the artists of the Belvedere and the empty, pathetic bombast of the men who glorified the Ring. This century encompasses an infinity of human striving. It begins with architecture and blossoms into music ; and the music of the high noon of Vienna and of the first decades of its decadence is one of the loftiest pinnacles of the European achievement. And nowhere more than in the work of the later 19th-century musicians can the spiritual agonies of decline be found more poignantly recorded. In the phrase " from Gluck to Mahler " is the story of slow physical exhaustion and spiritual complication.

THE MIDDLE DISTANCE

VI. SCHÖNBRUNN

IN these pages there have not been many dates;
perhaps there have been too few. Dates, however,
are the products of encyclopaedias, and in these may
be found in profusion. To the dryasdust every event,
no matter how small or how big, is a memorial to
the year it happened in; and thus in the books of
reference not a year that has passed but is on some
pretext recorded. To the English, too, every English
date, as such, is of more importance than any foreign
one. We are crammed with the dates of minor skir-
mishes, while the date of Rudolf Habsburg's final
victory over Ottokar of Bohemia, so decisive a day
for us all, is not remembered. If we had less dates
to recall there might seem more point in the few
that are worth recording.

For me, I believe for many of us, if we think a
moment, the solemnest, the most pathetic year in
all the history of our culture is the year 1791. What
the reference books have to say about it I do not
know; no doubt there was a battle or a treaty. But
we remember it here because it was the year of the
death of Mozart. He died on December 5th, on a
dirty, wintry night, in the Rauhensteingasse at the
heart of Vienna.

That is not all. It takes more than the death of a

genius to charge four ordinary figures with human significance. Bach, who was, if one can judge, a bigger man than Mozart, died in 1750, but his death did nothing to hallow that year. Shakespeare died in 1616, but that year remains without the least meaning or importance. The sad death of Mozart, on the other hand, not only removed from our world its most beautiful genius, it also set the seal on a process then lately begun which, continuing unchecked, has brought us where we are today. That process gained nothing by the date, but since we are human we clamour for a sign. Here is our sign.

The house in the Rauhensteingasse no longer stands, but the street itself remains, one of those deep, narrow streets which form the Inner City, running parallel to the Kärntnerstrasse and joining the Himmelpfortgasse, with its palace of Prince Eugene, to the Weihburggasse. If you continue up the Rauhensteingasse, along its extension, the Liliengasse, and across the Singerstrasse, you come in a few hundred yards to the Stefansplatz and the cathedral. Mozart when he died was Kapellmeister of the Stefansdom, in whose shadow he had so long lived—first in the Schulerstrasse, there composing *Figaro*, then in the street in which he died. One of his last thoughts had to do with that cathedral; this was that nobody should be told of his death until his friend Albrechtsberger, the academic master, could apply for the post which he alone should know was vacant.

Although the house where Mozart died no longer

stands—and if it did, who in the world could bear
to look at it?—there seems very little between us
and his death. It belongs to our world. The deep
past we have been able to view in solid blocks, as it
were, as one regards through glass the exhibits in a
museum. We can do that no longer; the birth of
Mozart took place in a vanished age, but his death
was the first unmistakable happening of our time,
and from now onwards past and present are so inextricably intertangled that we cannot hope to
separate them.

Mozart died alone and in bitter poverty. He was
the first great artist of our culture to die in this way.
The year was 1791. Nobody knows where his body
is. His coffin is lost among the coffins of the paupers
of Vienna. It was already thus lost a few weeks after
its interment. He was buried on December 6th;
the weather was still filthy; the way to the cemetery
was foul. Few followed the coffin, and these hurried
home. Mozart was quite alone in Vienna when he
died. Haydn was still living there, rather a fussy
old man. Beethoven was not to appear until the
following winter. Schubert was not yet born.

The death of Mozart in misery occurred when he
was thirty-five; he thus lived seven years longer
than Schubert, who also died in misery in Vienna.
But Schubert was a true child of the age, our age;
Mozart was not. His childhood, as everybody knows,
was brilliant and full of promise for the most successful future. He and his little sister were fêted in the
royal palaces of Europe; at Schönbrunn, the new
palace of Maria Theresa, which they also visited,

Mozart was smiled upon by Marie Antoinette.

But all that is over. Maria Theresa has been dead eleven years. Austria is shaking. Only a year ago the Emperor Joseph II, the People's Emperor, had lain down to die after rescinding most of his reforming edicts. His brother Leopold was on the throne in an attempt to pull together a disintegrating land. The age of rococo, which began with the building of Schönbrunn, is also dying, though it will linger, futilely, for many years. In this very year Marie Antoinette, now Madame Deficit, has been so insulted by the Parisian mob that her hair has turned white in a night ; and in a few months' time she will be dragged from her eminence and imprisoned until her death. But in Vienna Schönbrunn is still the focal point, and in the Hofburg, the shortest of walks from the dim house in the Rauhensteingasse, the Court continues in its amusements with all the splendour which the child Mozart had known. It is still a Court of music, some of it Mozart's own; but the great man there now is an Italian called Salieri, a pleasant mediocrity with a swollen head. In his last moments Mozart declares that Salieri has poisoned him.

But it is not to Salieri that we owe this pathetic difference between then and now. That springs from causes deeper and more august than anything embodied in a Court musician. And the pathos in this contrast is not the obvious thought of a great man dying miserably when he has enriched the world. The scene in the house in the Rauhensteingasse is unbearable in the moment; but there we have a great and sudden emotion of the kind that purges while it rends. The pathos is in the palace, with all that splendour vain and hollow because Mozart is not there, cannot be there, will never be there again in body or in spirit. That scene is full of a poignancy that can never be banished. For centuries society has been climbing, slowly toiling. A hundred years before it had reached an eminence, there building the Vienna of baroque. Obeying the universal law it sought to climb still higher; the aspiring fantasy of Fischer von Erlach broke into the exquisite flurry of rococo. Into that world the young Mozart came; his music of a youthful prodigy fitted his background to perfection. He was adored. But he also grew up and his music grew up with him. It passed the easy comprehension of his hearers. They were losing touch with the springs of vitality; those twining rococo tendrils of unparalleled elegance were too far removed from the sap of the tree of life and its greater branches. Fine and etiolated, they could not grow. But Mozart still grew. He tried to please. He could not. Unconsciously and against his will he was forced by some universal law from entertainment into prophecy. Prophets die alone. They are forced into being when a society is in decline.

Decadence may be defined in many ways, but this is its most striking and revealing feature—the metamorphosis of the artist from entertainer into prophet. The artist is always, in whatever phase of society, a creature of vitality. He is alive and growing. But in a healthy society others who are not artists are also alive, they grow with the artist, a little behind him, but understanding him; where he goes they are going. Then, later, when decline sets in, the artist still climbs, but the people have ceased to climb. His is no longer the voice of the people but that of a prophet crying alone. In the Vienna of our history that change took place gradually, almost imperceptibly to those participating in it (but so swiftly when seen from afar), in the latter part of the 18th century. Mozart, because he started so young, comprehended the transformation in his own development, experiencing in his lifetime the turning of the tide. When he died the ebb was set. Bach was never called upon to be a prophet, nor Handel, nor Gluck. Mozart was forced into that rôle uncomprehendingly and against his will. Beethoven was never anything else, nor has any other artist of genius been anything else since then —though in music, because music was then Vienna, and in Vienna, because of the swift pulse of its culture (the legacy, as we have seen, largely of its position as chief defender of the faith, for good and ill), the change is apparent earlier than in the other arts. . . . Since 1791, then. Has there ever been a more pathetic date? With it began the cult of great men, and implicit in that the ever-widening gulf between the people and the artist. Until today that fissure is so broad that it could swallow up a planet. It is nobody's fault. We all suffer for it, the artist too; but nobody can be blamed.

What I mean by prophecy in this context should be plain enough. I do not mean that the artist suddenly turned round, shook his fist at society and

predicted fire and brimstone for it. Some artists did;
it was in their temperament. Beethoven did, for
instance; and it was all part of the spirit of the time.
But Beethoven was not always self-conscious, and
Schubert never was; yet Schubert also was a prophet.
In his sublimest compositions we see the process very
clearly, uncomplicated as in Beethoven's work by
the individualistic challenge. We see, that is, a man
lonely in society dreaming of a beauty that arouses
little echo in the hearts of his contemporaries, and,
because he can find no response, gradually insulating
himself from the popular stimuli and plunging
ever more deeply into the depths of his own unique
spirit. There was no enthusiasm about the artist in
his acceptance of the prophetic mantle. At first, like
Mozart, he was unaware of its descent upon his
shoulders, and Mozart's contemporary, Haydn, was
never called upon to wear it. Beethoven knew it,
but in him we find very markedly the conflict between the prophet and the entertainer; he went
his own way most consciously, but he still expected
to be followed, and to some extent he was. Schubert
expected nothing. The process continued all through
the 19th century until in Gustav Mahler we find a
man no longer, as with Beethoven or Berlioz, chal-
lenging the world, but pursuing his way regardless,
or as regardless as one can be in face of hostile
demonstrations affecting one's very means of liveli-
hood. It is now that the legend of the artist in his
garret is established. The public expects. . .! Or,
from the point of view of the creator, art for art's
sake. The divorce is made absolute; it is an irrevoc-

able divorce. Bach would not have understood it, but Hindemith cannot get back to Bach.

Some pages back we spoke of a political revolution, the sudden increase in the power of ministers of the Crown, the new importance of the Viennese nobility, that going hand in hand with the flowering of baroque. We chose as our symbol of this revolution the Belvedere. But linked with this political revolution was a cultural one with similar manifestations. Until the 18th century the patronage of the arts had been the affair of the Crown. Apart from an occasional exaggerated gesture, such as the prostration of the Emperor Charles V before the painter Titian, the artist was an employee. Gifted men were recognised as such, but their gifts were a matter of degree, not of kind. There was no barrier drawn between the artist and the craftsman pure and simple, and none between the skilled craftsman and the ordinary man—perhaps because the ordinary man was never devoid of craftsmanship in some direction. Gifted men were recognised and venerated, but not as members of a class apart. The greatest painters of the Renaissance had their conceptions finished or even completely carried out by their pupils. Nobody objected. Today, when to praise an individual painter's brushwork is the critic's ultimate commendation, that seems incredible; but perhaps in those days good brushwork was taken for granted. Nor was that merely a freak of 15th-century Italians. Down to the day of Fischer von Erlach the artist was still regarded as a normal human being with particular gifts. Nobody in the world can have been more highly thought of by his contemporaries than Fischer von Erlach in Vienna, yet he too worked in the spirit of the Italian masters, collaborating freely with craftsmen and artists of lesser gifts. There were hundreds of them. It is difficult if not impossible to disentangle everywhere the work of von Erlach from the work of others. The great library in the Hofburg, which I purposely chose to illustrate as the finest of this architect's interiors, was never seen by him. The building of it was not commissioned until long after his death. The work was carried out by his son to the father's plans. Nobody knows what the son may have done to change his father's work. But the library remains a masterpiece of Fischer von Erlach. The arts were flourishing then; they were a popular expression; the artist was a man of talent, or even genius, with finer, maturer visions than his neighbours, but his neighbours immediately saw and *felt* what he was driving at and, given the word, could be relied upon to carry on. In music there was Gluck, who managed to entertain the Courts of Europe while effecting a revolution in the mode of opera. Bach in Saxony turned out his masterpieces for the benefit of an appreciative congregation in the course of his duties as organist and choirmaster at the Thomaskirche. In London Handel approached the theatre in the spirit of a Noel Coward, and did as well as a Noel Coward, relatively speaking; but what he wrote was *The Messiah* and *Acis and Galatea*, not *Bitter Sweet* and *Cavalcade*.

Do you still see no pathos in that wretched year,

the year of Mozart's death? He was the first great artist of our culture to die in squalor, neglected by his world. In that we see the writing on the wall, black and ineradicable, telling us once and for all that the children's children of the men who loved Handel and Gluck shall go for spiritual sustenance to Coward and Lehar. There is no going back; the process which has brought us to this place is not an arbitrary one to be reversed at will. There is the grandeur of inevitability about it, and contemplating that grandeur we may perhaps forget the pathos; we know that one day, in some other place, other Glucks and Handels will arise, they in their turn giving way to Cowards and Lehars. It is nobody's fault. You do not blame a man because he grows old, loses his teeth and then his faculties, has to be nourished on slops. The pathos is obvious and terribly oppressive—but there is also the grandeur of a system which we cannot understand, whose workings we call destiny; and I think the grandeur has it.

The political revolution in Vienna which put power into the hands of ministers and resulted in the Belvedere gave rise to a cultural revolution, resulting from the Belvedere. This shows the breaking of the Habsburg monopoly of the arts. The greatest art-collectors of the Viennese 18th century were not the Habsburgs, who by then had virtually completed the family collections which now fill the Art History Museum, but the Liechtensteins in their new palace, built for them by Fischer von Erlach

with fine painted ceilings by Pozzo and the most
beautiful stucco mouldings in the world; Haydn,
the greatest composer after Gluck (who had been
knighted by his emperor), was patronised not by
the Habsburgs but by the Hungarian Esterhazys.

Haydn was kept as a palace servant, dining in
the servants' hall, composing to his master's order.
Mozart also was kept as a servant by the Bishop of
Salzburg until he kicked against restraints and set
out to fend for himself—with what results we know.
Beethoven, by the weight of a formidable personality
combined with obvious if somewhat *outré* gifts,
somehow managed to hypnotise or bully his princes
and princesses into keeping him on his own terms.
Schubert was kept by nobody at all. He was the
first of the spare-time artists. Spare-time art—what
a phrase! Yet all art since Schubert, with the usual
exceptions—for some men are born with money,
some are amenable to rich old ladies, some have
luck, some have some incidental quality which
catches the fishy eye of the public at large—all art
since Schubert, with such odd exceptions, has been
spare-time art. There is your decadence. . . .

The men most gifted to create beauty have to
work at jobs they are not born for, jobs which could
be done by others without those rare gifts. Schubert
has to be a school-master or starve—he did first the
one, then, tiring of it, the other. Berlioz in France
has to fritter his energies away in journalism for
the daily papers. Wagner, whether one approves
of him or not, had gifts, and those gifts had to lie
neglected while he made piano arrangements of

inferior scores for hack publishers. We value our 19th-century art, or we say we do, the music, the painting, the writing. Yet all the 19th century would be barren of art if men here and there had not produced for us in their spare time and in face of every discouragement. No cat on the hearth, no slippers warmed by the fire for them.

The circumstances of the great masters, from Schubert onwards, are bad ; but to contemplate these alone gives us a wrong perspective. These great men are not art; they are merely the finest blooms of a stunted and neglected plant. It is the attitude of the public to the smaller men that most unambiguously displays our decadence. Today there is scarcely a composer or a writer or a painter possessing neither private means, nor the protection of an eccentric or a lost idealist, nor any curious quality which will please not only the more intelligent public but also the mob, who is not doing spare-time work. We may have no giants among us now ; but there are many who can create beauty in a small way. But these are not allowed to do so unless after office hours, when a man should be resting.

It is too late to do anything now, of course. The process has been going on since 1791. To expect an exhausted society to retain resilience and acuity would be too unreasonable. And, as we have said, it is too late. For so long has the artist been forced back on his own company that in sheer self-defence he has grown away from the world. The lack of a vital society to mirror forces the creator to explore

ever more deeply the individuality, and then to
exploit it. He can do nothing else. And when this
reaches a pitch, as it has in the work of many today,
the cleavage between the society and the individual
is too great to be bridged by anything at all. Public
and artist get at cross-purposes, hurl mud at each
other, then die—each with the dignity of an ex-
piring frog.

It is too late to do anything now. One hardly
knows whether one would if one could. One does
not tamper idly with destiny. And this process, this
decline, has given us so much beauty. Whether a
healthy beauty or not is neither here nor there.
This process of decadence is no more voluntary
on our part than the process of infection is on the
part of a consumptive. He has his visions and his
heightened sensibility denied to the healthy man;
he does not question the validity of these, he accepts
them as he accepts the inevitability of the disease,
regarding them in some way as compensation for
the horror. That is not to say that those of us who
still feel in our veins some tingle of survived vitality
should rush to embrace the more marked manifestations of corruption. On the contrary.

But although it is too late to alter things now,
and although nobody can be blamed for the universal
softening of the brain which has left those with
vitality nothing to explore but themselves and
brought dictators into power in some countries and
in others bankers, with the consequent enslavement
of the millions, it is as well to know and recognise
the symptoms. In the human being age strutting

as masqueraded youth is ridiculous and horrible
to see, but no less absurd, no less horrible, is the
sight of a society which purblindly refuses to realise
its years.

This chapter is headed Schönbrunn and the title
is not so far-fetched or perverse as might appear
from the preceding pages. In England we refuse not
merely to grow old gracefully but even to realise that
years may count at all. In Vienna we have our
opposite. Vienna, instinctively intent on poise and
dignity of manner, determined at all costs to preserve her grace, has let herself grow old too soon.
That is a fault like any other; but we at least may
learn from it. I have called this chapter Schönbrunn
because with the building of that palace Vienna
scaled the peak of her maturity, upon which she
has ever since languished.

It was started under the dull and undistinguished
Charles VI, author of the Pragmatic Sanction, which
was designed to secure the succession for his own
children, male, female, or idiot, and at one time,
between two treaties, an enthusiastic king of Spain.
It was started to the designs of Fischer von Erlach,
then discontinued, then taken up again by Maria
Theresa, who made it her summer residence.
Although the new architect, Pacassi, was not a man
of genius, he made of this palace a place always imposing and lovely enough in parts. It is enormous. It
is, remember, the Habsburg reply to the Bourbons,
with whom they were at loggerheads. It has a
frontage of 220 yards; it contains 1441 rooms and

139 kitchens (whether the 1441 is inclusive or exclusive of kitchens I do not know); it stands in a
park of 495 acres (Hyde Park is 100 acres smaller)
which includes a zoo, a botanical garden and a palm-
house 100 feet high. I supply these statistics, hot
from Baedeker, because nothing else can convey
the scale. They do not, however, evoke the image;
to do that adequately, indeed, one needs to be a
Canaletto.

One reaches this place by proceeding from the
Hofburg along the Mariahilfestrasse, which is two
and a half miles long and thus extends from the
limits of the Inner City to the outer and fashionable
suburbs full of pleasant villas which lie sheltered
by the Wienerwald. It is not a beautiful street; we
leave the 18th century with the low and rambling
stuccoed stables of the Hofburg, which lie behind
the twin museums of art and natural history, en-
countering it again only when we reach Schönbrunn
itself. What lies between is of the 19th century,
affording proof of the international nature of that
blight and yet, with unexpected and refreshing
flashes, showing how Vienna never utterly suc-
cumbed. This is the bourgeois shopping centre; it
is hard to remember that twenty years ago it was
still also the Imperial carriage-way linking the
winter with the summer palace. Originally, of
course, it cut across green fields, making quite a
pretty drive.

At the end of this drabness the palace appears as
a sudden vision from another world—or, rather, we
seem miraculously to emerge from another world,

our world of mercantile drabness, into *the* world. We have not so long ago left the Hofburg, remember; and the Ringstrasse, though bogus, is in the grand manner with the sort of air which the 19th century did not often achieve. At any rate, Schönbrunn lies before us with an air of invincible, unquestionable permanency, aloof and superbly at ease, prepared to stay there quietly sprawling in the sun for as many generations as people care to jerry-build and haggle with tinned goods, not implying reproach of these activities but utterly oblivious of them. The only thing is that from the moment we set eyes on that monstrous façade to the moment we turn our pigmy backs on it we are completely dominated by it, forced to detach ourselves for just so long from whatever 20th-century preoccupations we may be harbouring. Some of us of course need only the least encouragement to cast down our burdens with relief; others, with more faith in their rôle as children of progress and the light, do not give in without a struggle; but by the end they must feel very brow-beaten.

The colour is yellowish, or beige. One turns from the drab main road and skirting an uninteresting park, rather like the Green Park, approaches a huge and, for the moment, indeterminate block; then, crossing the Wien, that historical small river which here flows visibly, one comes face to face with the whole immense conception. Beyond a wrought-iron gateway, flanked by two tall obelisks each surmounted with a gilded eagle; beyond again a desert-like gravelled forecourt, with mounting-blocks and lamp-posts symmetrically disposed, is reared this

low but cliff-like, fantastically long, yellowish expression of Maria Theresa's faith in her family's
future. Isolated in that mighty courtyard, regarded
blankly by serried tiers of windows, forty to each
row, one instantly succumbs. There is a brief moment
of protest. One realises that Pacassi was not equal
to this task, that, however brave a front he may have
put on it when in conference with his mistress or
her agents, he must (unless he was a bigger fool
than one imagines) have spent sleepless nights
wondering what on earth he could do to make 200
yards of frontage dignified yet interesting. One
recalls the massive grandeur of the palace of the
Hungarian Lifeguards in the Hofstallstrasse, the
superb doorway of the Bohemian Palace with its
spread the width of three windows, its caryatids,
its capping splendours of heraldry and clouds, and
sighs that Fischer von Erlach was not allowed to
finish the task he had begun. One recalls that miracle
of lightness, the Belvedere, and wonders whether
Hildebrandt, given Pacassi's chance, could not have
made of one of the greatest palaces in Europe also
its crowning monument to human fantasy. . . . But
the protest dies on the lips. Pacassi is not a genius,
but what he has created—the light yet curiously
stilted effect of the central block which breaks the
roof-line of the horizontal mass, memorable for the
precise ceremonial of its double staircase curving
round to the first-floor balcony above the main
entrance—all this, precisely through its clipped
imagination, most perfectly expresses the Habsburgs
of our time who were to live there, be born there,

o

die there, and finally, deserted in those endless corridors, there sign the document of abdication which meant their end.

One walks straight through that astonishing wall, in beneath the double staircase, through the thickness of the palace, and out on to the gravel expanse and the gardens which face south. The palace is then seen to be built at the foot of a sloping hill; the eye is drawn over the flat gardens and upwards to the summit of the hill on which is perched a Gloriette, an open-sided colonnaded hall, surmounted by winged statuary, which from this distance looks delicate and airy. The hill itself is a swelling grassy slope, divided from the palace area by a low wall which backs a fountain of an elaboration worthy of Versailles, the Fountain of Neptune with all the allegorical figures of the sea. Fringing this wall, on the farther side of it, is a sparse, irregular line of trees, mostly small firs, which produce at the heart of all this artificiality an effect of delicate piquancy. Flanking the swelling close-clipped hillside are dense plantations of deciduous trees growing naturally; but lining the level gardens between the palace and the hill are the tall, square-clipped hedges of the 18th-century mode, the dark foliage picked out by statues placed in small embrasures. The gardens themselves are geometrical in plan, sharp colour massed in flower-beds of all shapes and sizes making a complicated pattern with the shorn grass verges and wide gravel paths.

That is what one sees. Only a small acreage is comprised in those gardens which are visible from

the palace steps; there is much else besides, gardens
in all the *genres* of gardening, leafy retreats cooled
by fountain-jets; but the impression is all we require, and this is the impression; the stilted,
angular ceremony, not untouched by grace, of the
monstrous palace harmonising to perfection with
the stiff, sharp-toned formality of the immediate
gardens. The terraced gardens of the Belvedere are
warm and eager in comparison.

This is beauty of a curious kind, thin, perhaps,
but cooling to the brain. The effect depends a great
deal on the fantastic scale. Great crowds, dispersing,
can lose themselves here ; the Viennese took the
tram to Schönbrunn when Franz Josef lived and
worked there (for this strange family has always
been free-handed with its property, provided the
ultimate ownership was understood); they continue
to do so today; it is to be hoped that they will for
ever. It is impossible not to believe that close and
intimate acquaintanceship with such a mood can
fail as an influence towards fineness. People who
live among the mountains, it is said in contradiction
of this argument, fail to reflect in their characters
the majesty and grandeur of their perpetual environment. The answer to that is that it is by no
means true of all of them, and, for the rest, inbreed-
ing has a lot to answer for. The Viennese, whatever
their sins, are not inbred. And, of course, their
trouble is largely that they have had too much of
Schönbrunn: it is not, from the point of view of the
élan vital, a good thing to be enabled to escape at
will from the oppression of a bungled present into

the dream realisation of the past, when that past is strong enough to make the present seem unreal. However, one inclines to the belief that it is better to have too much of a good thing than too much of a bad thing; and Schönbrunn, when all is said, is— by city standards—good: it at least is the extremely positive expression of a respectable point of view— that which regards the triumph of man over nature as the supreme felicity.

The exterior of Schönbrunn Palace, though not lacking in fineness, scarcely prepares one for the rioting extravagance concealed by that cool and non-committal front. In these rooms, or at least in the more famous of the one thousand four hundred and forty-one, we have the apotheosis of rococo in Vienna, matched only by Maria Theresa's own additions to the Hofburg—such as the ballroom with the Gobelins where we had our glimpse of *Figaro*. Maria Theresa is too often painted as a great bene-volent solemnity, made hard by her twin and mutually helpful faiths of Family and Religion. We are to see her standing aloof from the mood of her age, which was licentious as to morals, rococo as to architecture—or vice versa. No one would dream of denying her goodness or her amazing strength. Her morals must have been the boast of the Church of Rome; though fearing childbirth as nothing else she bore sixteen children to an inconstant husband and no breath of scandal ever touched her. But this is a most inadequate picture. Educated not as an heir presumptive but as a marriageable princess, not troubling as a young girl even to feign an interest

Rococo at Schönbrunn

The Great Gallery, Schönbrunn

in politics, she yet, when called, showed herself the most stubborn Habsburg of them all. She bore those children to her husband, but she also ruled him utterly; what is more, with complete awareness of his moral lapses which were very much at odds with her private code, she continued to love him. The years of her maturity were weighed down by the most complicated worries of state, yet she never forgot how to behave like a woman when the moment called for it. For a woman of these strong and apparently conflicting characteristics to be a dullard is unthinkable. Her biographers should look a second time. . . . And then there is this palace. This, and everything she built, took on the shape of the most involved and extravagant rococo fancy. She need not have built like that. She had supreme command. Rococo is not even baroque, which, however fantastic, is founded in serious purpose; rococo is elegant fantasy and nothing more. One of the illustrations to this book is of the Oval Chinese Cabinet at Schönbrunn—a tall room in the shape of an oval, decorated with an endless system of gilded, creeping, tendrilled foliage. The whole room, the ceiling and the walls, is netted in by this artificial growth intertwined with an extreme of symmetrical and exuberant intricacy. On the ceiling gilded peacocks cling to the furiously branching scrollwork; the walls are lined with mirrors of elaborate shapes framed by leaping tendrils; great Chinese vases stand on the patterned parquet floor; lesser vases in profusion are upheld against the walls by elaborate sconces fancifully growing outwards from the gilded

tracery; from the ceiling hangs the most exquisite
of chandeliers, a burst of foliage, tortuously wrought,
surmounted by a head of gilded flowers. What
serious purpose lies behind this fancy? What is there
there but high-spirited delight in an imagination
set free? And this was the room chosen by Maria
Theresa for the meetings of her Privy Council.

It is not what one would expect either from the
somewhat precise exterior of the palace or from
knowledge of the later Habsburgs, with whom that
exterior is more in keeping. What one would expect
is the kind of thing one finds at Versailles, a replica
of the hugely overrated *Salle des Glaces*, where
fancy is struck dead by megalomania. Instead, the
show-piece of Schönbrunn, the *Grosse Galerie*, is,
for all its requisite formality, a place of human
warmth and loveliness, conceived in the same spirit
as the Redoutensaal in the Hofburg, a pastel of
white and gold with mirrors used discreetly, the
walls brilliant with a thousand candle sconces,
massy chandeliers suspended from a warmly painted
ceiling.

There are other rooms, nearly fifteen hundred
of them, but we cannot look at them all. These two
give us our mood, others may give us history; for
the whole story of the dissolution of the Habsburg
monarchy is written in Schönbrunn—from the
Napoleon Room, where the invading conqueror,
making Schönbrunn his headquarters, slept while
attending to business in the city, to the all too-
celebrated bedroom of Franz Josef, cell-like, with
its iron bedstead (upholstered by solicitous members

of the Household with a feather-bed) in which the
old man, to his great good fortune, died two years
before the deluge, to the Blue Room with its Chinese
wallpaper where the young Emperor Karl, alone
in this monstrous and deserted shell, watched over
by two guards whom nobody came to relieve, signed
the instrument of abdication : " Now as ever filled
with unalterable affection for My peoples, I will not
let Myself be a hindrance to their free development".

Those words do not ring true to Habsburg type.
They, more than the actual overthrow which they
acknowledge, signal the end. It is impossible, suddenly, in the 20th century, to introduce the spirit
of that statement into a form of government
shackled to a distant past. Other Habsburgs would
have run from Schönbrunn, and considerably more
promptly than Karl, but they would not have talked
like that. For the Habsburg policy, as Hermann
Bahr has observed, was continually to *mould* their
subjects ; and what they could not mould they broke.
Land and religion were the two sustaining interests ;
the subject peoples could do what they liked so long
as the Habsburgs had the land and so long as they
behaved like good Catholics. This moulding process,
and, failing malleability in the subject, breaking, is,
as others have pointed out, with other influences
which we have touched on, responsible for much
of the softness of the Viennese. In the days of the
counter-reformation the staunchest and most independent spirits were killed or driven into exile
rather than renounce their principles ; in the days

of Metternich the most perilous occupation was intellectual exercise; all through history, then, men with influence and power have been the most ardent of the Patriots for Me—Bohemians, Hungarians, Poles, that is to say, who put personal advancement in the shadow of the Habsburg double-headed eagle above their racial loyalties and ties. These men led the society of Vienna—not good Poles and Bohemians but, in some ways, renegades. By no means all were bad, or even weak; many, no doubt, supported by conviction the Imperial arms. More, however, did not.

And even when a Habsburg chose to be enlightened, like the liberal Joseph, son, successor, and *enfant terrible* of Maria Theresa, he was not content to leave people to themselves. "All that is over!" was Joseph's favourite phrase, and woe betide the citizen who failed to realise that he meant it. He offered them wine instead of water; but even the rarest vintage may appear a mixed blessing when it is forced down one's throat at all hours of the day, leaving one with no alternative but to drink it or die of thirst. How much better might Austria have been for an occasional King Log; the Habsburgs, whatever their faults, were rarely that.

Karl's farewell confession of love for his people (and that, I believe, was not the conventional phrase it might have been on the lips of Franz Josef, secure on his throne, addressing a deputation from the backwoods of Transylvania) was by no means the first sign of an anachronistic softening of the Habsburg grip—it had been an iron hand in an iron

glove, and no matter now how limp the hand lay
in the glove, so long as that existed, rusted and long
set, it could not diminish its pressure. Romantic
ideas had appeared in that family some fifty years
before, in Rudolf, Franz Josef's only son and also in
Franz Josef's brother, Maximilian. It is idle to specu-
late as to whether, if the father had died sooner and
the son had lived longer, there would have been a
European War or not. The whole Habsburg history
of this time seems to reveal nothing so much as the
decision of destiny that there must be a European
cataclysm, and that decision was reinforced and
rendered ineluctable by every conceivable means.
The blindness of Fate in this context takes on a new
complexion. That blindness is usually taken to mean
a randomness, a careless wantonness. But here one
is struck, looking back, less by an inattentive cruelty
than by a blind and superhuman determination to
secure by some means, any means, at any cost, a
definite end. That end was the breakdown of an effete
Europe by the precipitation of a war—or the regenera-
tion of an effete Europe by a purge of war and chaos
—whichever way you choose to look at it. We can
see the devious workings in other lands, but in
Austria, in every matter slightly over life-size, the
spectacle is at its clearest. We have on the throne a
man who could both unconsciously precipitate and
then, still more or less unconsciously, sanction such
a war. He is human and he may die. He is surrounded by figures imbued with a new spirit, who,
if given the chance, may be able to spin things out
to a still more attenuated length. The first is the

son, the Crown Prince of Austria-Hungary. He dies by his own hand. The second is the brother, next in the Succession, the weak and obstinate idealist, Maximilian. He dies before a firing-squad in Mexico. The third is the Queen, a romantic Wittelsbach, beautiful, slightly mad, living in frenzied opposition to all that Habsburg stands for. She dies at the hand of an Italian assassin. The fourth is the unprepossessing unknown quantity, the nephew, Franz Ferdinand, who also has unorthodox ideas. He dies at the hand of Gavrilo Princip, and, what is more, his death unchains the furies.

To some it may seem childish, but in face of these four violent deaths which overtook in so short a span four Habsburgs, each with new ideas, each with an influence on the supreme power, one may be pardoned for seeing, or imagining one sees, the workings of a force of irresistable impetus, moving ruthlessly towards an envisaged end, blind only in so far as it shows a disregard of detail, removing everything, *everything*, that might conceivably obstruct its purpose, in the spirit of a Herod come to slaughter. That at least is the effect when, wise after the event, one can look back far enough. I leave it to philosophers and theologians to explain away, if indeed they wish to, the pregnant coincidences which comprise the whole of history. I know nothing of causation, or the absence of it. I do not, as these pages some time ago disclosed, believe that the abdication of Edward VIII of England was caused by the unwise marriage of a 16th-century Habsburg. All these things in themselves are trivial and acci-

dental ; but they are accidental to some profound
activity, or process, incessantly working in accordance with what statesmen once upon a time called
the long view and have lately reduced to five-year
plans ; they are symptomatic ; they reveal the
direction of the process as mounds of thrown-up
earth reveal the subterranean progress of the mole.
One can see what ground has been covered, but one
cannot predict where the next mound will be ; one
can only make one's guesses, which are likely to be
wrong.

However—when the head of a great House has
to choose between the throne and his personal inclinations and ends by following the latter (I refer
to the Crown Prince Rudolf), one may take it as
symptomatic of a swift disintegration of the *status
quo*. Rudolf committed suicide in 1889, two years
before the centenary of Mozart's death. The writing
on the wall in 1791 can have been visible only to
the clearest-sighted eyes, and then only obscurely ;
it is plain enough to us in the light of our own slant-
ing rays. But during the century that intervened
between the death of a neglected genius and the
suicide of a Habsburg crown prince the time-spirit
had been active. Many things had happened. Joseph
had carried out his dictatorial revolution which included the suppression of the Jesuits. Francis I and
Metternich between them had answered this with
their bloodless but blighting counter-reformation,
the one bringing back the Jesuits to their old familiar
regnancy, the other suppressing speech and paralys-
ing thought. Then Metternich himself had ended in

the revolt of 1848 which frightened Franz Josef into his undying abhorrence of the mob. The walls by then were covered with writings, all saying the same thing but in different ways, so that each man at that uneasy banquet should read in his own language the message that touched his own interest. Franz Josef saw his message.

Then, with the suicide of Rudolf, the walls themselves were seen to totter; few could miss that dreadful movement. An empire had been built and then upheld by a chain of monarchs who, no matter how they panted for power, were ruled also by a sense of duty and responsibility which might operate in different ways in different men but was inviolate and inviolable—until 1889. Their duty entailed the suppression of many personal inclinations, if it also at times was the pretext for yielding to personal manias. The greatest article of statesmanship was marriage. Marriage was the begetter of two necessary properties, new lands, new heirs. With this ideal in mind the number of families eligible to provide an archduke with a wife were embarrassingly limited. By the time of Franz Josef new lands were not so simply to be come by in this way. One married into certain families still, either for the sake of a political alliance, or else simply because after cen-turies of domination it was unthinkable to marry beyond the exalted circle. That is decadence, the upholding, at great inconvenience, of an old tradi-tion from which the meaning has departed. But it is inevitable. A 15th-century Habsburg would have cheerfully married a scullery-maid had she been

able to bring Hungary with her ; a 19th-century
Habsburg would sooner have married the most
dowerless and degenerate princess than a commoner,
though she were of ancient family, beautiful,
accomplished, rich beyond all dreams, and the
bringer of an alliance with all the Americas. It is
inevitable.

The young Rudolf himself, brilliant, liberal-
minded, obstinate, unstable (the character came
of the cross between the dour, tenacious Habsburgs
and the mad, passionate ardour of the Wittelsbach
blood of that unhappy queen and mother), was
himself well married according to plan. His wife
was a princess of Belgium, bigoted, unimaginative,
not unnaturally jealous. Marriage, as hitherto, was
an affair of state ; love one found, if one could, with
mistresses. Rudolf was Habsburg enough to recognise
that necessity and submit to it. Married, unhappy
and distrait, he had many mistresses ; he seemed to
take his pleasures lightly, turning to them in reckless relief from the barrenness of his own domestic
life, the stilted narrowness of that Spanish Court
and his burning political preoccupations ; for he,
like Joseph II but perhaps with more imagination
and truer fire, lived only for the moment when he
too could say " All that is over ! " and be obeyed.
So long as his father remained alive and active he
had to wait ; to kill time he threw himself at
pleasure's head and conspired a little with the
advanced minds of his day—how much we do not
know.

All we do know is that suddenly he fell in love,

and with a young girl, Marie Vetsera. According to all reports she was charming, beautiful, accomplished, gay; she was a baroness belonging to the upper middle-classes, mingling through her parents with the higher world, but forbidden access to Court for lack of the sixteen quarterings; she lived with her parents in the Salesianergasse, between the Rennweg and the Stadtpark, on the edge of that quarter of palaces and gardens which centres on the Belvedere. Little enough in the way of facts is known about this affair; it is not our purpose to make a reconstruction in the modern manner of the tragedy of this young girl—for tragedy it was; that has been attempted by various writers with varying degrees of impertinence. We recapitulate the salient facts because that tragedy was also in deed if not in chronology the end of the Habsburgs as a ruling house. Meeting at some state ball the two fell in love and Rudolf, now as stubborn as he had been unstable, was not content to make her his mistress ; he wished to divorce his wife and marry her. Secretly he wrote to the Pope for a dispensation, but the Pope consulted his champion, the Emperor. The consequent scene between father and son must have had an intolerable poignancy ; both men were speaking from their hearts and both were Habsburgs : and, in the 19th century, one could only be an absolute monarch by forgetting that one had a heart. It was a call to duty on the part of the ancient, foundering order to the one man who could redeem it. Some days later, at the Prince's hunting-box at Mayerling in the wooded hills to the south-west of

Vienna, Rudolf was found dead, shot through the head, beside the body of Marie Vetsera, which was covered with flowers.

There was to be no rejuvenation after all and the end was starkly in sight. Faced with a calamity which not only shook its foundations but was also liable to sully its clear name, the crumbling house of Austria had a spasmodic access of panic strength which took the form of a bitter lapse into mediaeval brutality. The young girl was dragged in the mud and her harmless memory befouled. The supreme forces of a mighty empire were directed to her entire obliteration, in vain. The lovers were not buried, as requested, side by side. The body of Rudolf was laid in state and then, with all the black and Spanish ceremony which he had loathed in life, solemnly interred in the Habsburg vault of the Kapuchinerkirche. Marie Vetsera was left as she lay, untended and unguarded; the fact that a Habsburg had given his life for her sake was neither here nor there. Then, in the dead of night, in accordance with the Imperial command, she was visited by two of her uncles, her body was clothed; carried upright between the two men she was taken downstairs and then placed, fully dressed, upright in an open carriage, supported by her uncles, masquerading as a living figure. They took her to a near-by burial ground. The world heard nothing of this gruesome farce for many years. Six months later the Emperor caused a letter to be written to the young girl's mother : " Deeply as His Majesty deplores the wounds which may have been inflicted upon the heart of a desolated mother by the arrangements made for the interment of her unhappy daughter it is necessary, nevertheless, to take into account the indescribable confusion which reigned at the scene of the catastrophe, the rapidity with which decisions had to be made, and the urgency of what measures were decided on ".

It was time the Habsburgs ended. Deeply as we deplore the suppressed agony of mind which a desolated and not ungallant Emperor was called upon to endure, caused not only by the personal tragedy, but also by the collapse of a tradition and a heritage which he had suffered so much to uphold, it is necessary, nevertheless, to take into account the fact that for good or ill the times were changing, that a new code of decency, vague, sentimental, often ridiculous, but containing the germ of goodness, was taking shape, and that people who cannot exist without savagely affronting the best and most valuable elements of a new spirit have to go.

They went.

Whether or not the tragic outcome of the love of Rudolf for Marie Vetsera was wholly due to that love it is impossible to say. Or, rather, one can say surely enough that it was not; what we cannot know is how much it was not, to what extent the suicide was influenced by politics. That the Prince's fatal state of mind, his pessimism, was induced as much by frustrated political ideals as by the hopelessness of his love is evident; but there are also reports that he was up to his neck in conspiracies against the

established order as represented by his father, and
this seems not unlikely. Certainly some of his known
actions would, had they been discovered at the time,
have been regarded by the Emperor as nothing but
sedition. More than that we do not know—the
present writer does not know, that is; some may
and doubtless do; but for the outsider there remains,
still firm after all these years, a barrier hindering
close enquiry into the life of that unhappy prince.
The Habsburgs, emperors or not, are loyal to their
family.

But even were it established today beyond all
doubt that a prime motive for the suicide was political it would not alter the sad significance of Mayerling; and that tiny village on the western slopes
of a wooded spur of the Wienerwald, with Rudolf's
shooting-box now used as a Carmelite nunnery (the
Catholic sense of humour either does not exist or else
is so subtle and at the same time so audacious that
it makes the non-Catholic gasp) and the room where
he died as a chapel, has a strong fascination and the
power to fill the visitor with an emotion of a singu-
larly complex kind. The darkness of the woods is
unrelieved; the sunlight only emphasises it.

Not that that place matters, really, one way or
the other. It is hardly guessing to say that Rudolf's
life would have ended in catastrophe, sooner or later.
In 1889 he was burnt up with impatience, exhausted
with dissipation, becoming more reckless each day;
but the Emperor Franz Josef, the cause of all the
agonising, was to live for another twenty-seven
years. In 1916, the year of his father's death at the

age of eighty-six, Rudolf would have been, had he lived, a prematurely aged man of fifty-eight—and already at thirty-one he was at breaking point. One way or another calamity must have come. Nor was the rot confined to the heart of one man; there was at that time a stirring among the Habsburg able-bodied males. A rift had shown itself. On the one side was the old order typified strongly enough by the Emperor's rigid pedantry and preoccupation with small matters, but even more strongly in the savagely reactionary Uncle Albrecht with his ape-like countenance; on the other side was a certain eager, liberal-minded warmth, allied with weakness, and typified by the Archduke Salvator, who schemed, resigned his privileges, married into the bourgeoisie and was admired by his cousin Rudolf. This movement was inevitable. Life at Court was pursued on the excessively rigid lines laid down by the Spanish Court of the 16th century. The Empress Elizabeth, who must have been a trying woman for all her beauty and charm, dashed wildly against the bars, breaking her heart. The preservation of etiquette had degenerated into a private game for degenerate courtiers, who could be as rude as they liked to anyone who broke the rules, even to the Empress. Elizabeth was a romantically minded woman and a brave one. The things she did which turned the Court against her were almost invariably harmless and often laudable and salutary. Her love of horses, for instance, drove her to the companion-ship of the grooms in the Imperial stables. But everything she did, going her own way, was done with a Teutonic tactlessness which always put her in the wrong and only increased the circumambient rigidity. No wonder the younger Habsburgs had had enough.

One of the most delightful of all interludes in contemporary Vienna is furnished by an hour or two spent at the Spanish Riding School in the Hofburg. Here in a great baroque hall of extreme loveliness, all white, we assist at a ceremonial of the 17th century. To the accompaniment of familiar and anachronistic music played simply, perhaps by a little band of horns and trumpets, the stallions of an ancient stable of unparalleled purity go through all the exercises of the *haute-école*. The arena of tan, or sawdust, is cleared save for two stout wooden posts set upright a few feet apart and painted with spiral stripes like barbers' poles. The band strikes up a fanfare and then there enters a small and stately procession composed of men on horseback dressed in cocked hats, brown coats and white buckskin breeches. The horses are the most beautiful animals in the world, pure white, coal black or dapple-grey. All have flowing tails, small heads, arched necks; all pick up their feet with exquisite precision and dancing lightness. These are the youngest stallions of the Lippizaner stud. Slowly, solemnly, they show their paces and are taken away. They have fantastic names : Pluto Mercurio, Maestoso Africa, Maestoso Theodorasta, Neapolitano Virtuosa, Neapolitano Montenueva, Favory Montenegra, Conversano Presciana. They are housed in the neighbouring stables, where they may be visited and patted, superb and palpable visitants from another world. Before they are ready for the *tours de force* of the *haute-école* they must undergo years of steady training at the hands of the men in brown coats and white breeches with their Czech, Hungarian and German names. This development in all its phases we now see embodied in the accomplishments of senior animals. The painted posts are brought into play; standing between them, attached by two leathers, the shining animals obey the crack of a whip or a monosyllabic command and go with astounding deliberacy through the stilted, artificial poses, reminiscent in all their magnificent and nervous muscularity of the bronze horses of renaissance sculptors; the posts are abandoned, and they weave and interweave in a polka or quadrille to the music of Strauss or Lanner, which, anywhere else, would be offensively anachronistic, but which, in Vienna, where anachronism is unknown because the whole of life is based on it, merely adds to the artificial charm. Finally, when everything seems to have been shown and proved, comes the majestic climax, the *Schulen über der Erde* executed by the veterans, and here we have all the fantastic positions of the classical school displayed to perfection—from the *Levade*, familiar through countless equestrian statues, that rigid pose of an animal rearing from its haunches, as it were, the hind-legs almost parallel with the ground, the fore-legs beating the air, drawn close in to the massive chest, to the most elaborate and impossible flourish, the *Capriole*, a leap upwards but not forwards from the standing position, the back straight, the neck arched, the fore-legs drawn up beneath the chest, the hind-legs lashing out beneath the flowing tail. . . .

This is the fruit of an unbroken tradition extending through five centuries, surviving the Habsburg *débâcle*. The horses we see today are said to be the direct descendants of the original animals brought from Naples in the 17th century. The ceremonial is certainly the same. And in this fantastic conservatism of the *haute-école*, practised, as nowhere else, in the heart of 20th-century Vienna (a city which has as little use for horses as New York), we see, perfectly mirrored, the conservatism of the last Imperial Court. The cabrioling of the pure white Lippizaners is, by all our standards, the absolute of uselessness. The horses, fine, beautiful and strong, are utterly divorced from all natural movement, living their lives in an atmosphere of unreality with every step laid down for them and no chance whatsoever of a moment's deviation. And so it was with the 19th-century Habsburgs.

Meaningless conservatism governing the life of a stud of thoroughbreds is one thing; it provides a glorious spectacle; it even ensures that somewhere in the world there shall be men who know all there is to know of riding. It is good for such knowledge to be preserved if nobody is injured by the manner of its preservation. But applied to the life of a ruling family it is quite another thing. The Court, intent on *caprioles* and *ballotades*, was lost to all reality. It was very much on show, but the motions through

which it went were meaningless to the onlooker
and mechanical to the performer, who might as well
have been dead.

The position of the Court of Vienna during the
last phase of the monarchy was indeed peculiar. It
was, in a way, far more open to popular inspection
than, say, the Court of St. James, yet at the same
time infinitely farther removed from popular feeling. Commoners had easy access to its corridors.
Every day the band played and the guard was
changed in the vast parade-ground before the Burg.
That happens in London still, but as a formality ;
in Vienna it provided a spectacle for the Emperor
which could be shared by his subjects, and these
knew that every morning Franz Josef left his study
table to look down with pride and affection on the
spectacle below. And when the Hungarian Life
Guards, Maria Theresa's Own, marched off to the
baroque palace by Fischer von Erlach which was
their barracks, not one of them below the rank of
captain, all of them shining in their scarlet jackets,
plumes and yellow boots, the leopard skin slung across
their shoulders, the housings of their chargers green,
the people knew that their Emperor was delighting
in their glitter no less than they; it was an intimate
Court ceremonial, open to all. The Court was always
with the people, yet infinitely remote. Night after
night at the Imperial Opera or the Burgtheater on
the Ring the Emperor could be seen in his box,
drinking in the same spectacle, enjoying the same
music at the same moment as the poorest of his
subjects ; but the apparent intimacy was a fraud.

The British royal family has a private life, inviolable
as the private lives of all its subjects; save on official
occasions the King and Queen are not a great deal
on view. The Viennese knew far more of the interior
economy of the Hofburg and Schönbrunn than we
know of Buckingham Palace and Windsor. The
ruling house of England shares to an infinitely less
extent than that of Austria in the finer social
activities of their subjects; it might well share more.
It is, nevertheless, infinitely closer to the people *in
their lives.*

A curious atmosphere prevailed in Imperial
Vienna; the people led their lives in the shadow of
a mighty Court which could always be seen but
which never saw. The Court was a mountain-peak,
soaring above the valley, fascinating and romantic,
yet unscalable. Or, one is reminded of a stern and
rigorous Victorian *mauvais père de famille*, always
on show save in certain secret moments, always
immaculate in shining side-whiskers and brushed
frock-coat, always making pronouncements to which
there was no reply. The children see him frequently,
but he does not see them—unless they are dis-
obedient, arousing thunder ; they bask in his
splendour, never daring to raise their voices, and,
when the impossible back is turned, proceed with
their private games and whisperings—which are
all the more private because one can never be
certain that the demi-god may not suddenly turn
in one's direction, and probably all the more silly. . . .

All this had to go, *had* to go. It went at Mayerling

on a winter's day, the 30th of January, 1889.

And although it might equally well have gone at any other time or place there is a certain magic in locality, and the chilly spell of the forest trees, dark and unregarding on their crowded hill-tops, is not diminished by our knowledge. In this loneliness the spirit of an ancient family was broken. That was the climax of the play. The denouement took place at Schönbrunn.

VII. THE RING

WE were sitting—it seems a very long time ago —at our ease in one of a thousand coffee-houses, cooled by a gentle breeze which eddied in through the window spaces, drinking the coffee of our choice, one of those innumerable varieties which you ask for by name, never specifying coffee, *sui generis*. We started comfortably moralising—about the future of Europe, or whatever—and that, per-versely, sent us traipsing off to explore the embodied past. We have seen a good deal, far more than we have recorded, for every separate excursion has taken us past aspects either new or changing to the second glimpse. We have perambulated through time with scarcely a glance at the teeming life around us ; but if we have ignored the living, shouldering them aside to get a view of the dead, we have at least by now some faint conception of their background, which is what we wanted ; for men and women seen without the background from which they have gradually, through centuries, advanced, have no more significance than so many marionettes. And from now on, until the last of these pages and then beyond the covers of this book, we are free to live in the present; for Vienna *has* a present, although, as I have said, it is so intertwined with the past that it is difficult to separate the two. That present has a beauty of its own, but it is static, it does not advance ; it is symbolised, in more senses than one and with dazzling aptness, by a Ring, a closed circle.

One of the first things that presented itself to our eyes was just that great street, or boulevard, called the Ringstrasse. Since that early moment we have crossed it and recrossed it countless times, in pursuit of this or that illusion, but, save for an occasional sneer, we have ignored it—and with surprising success, it seems, looking back : I should never have thought it possible to spend so much time in Vienna without being caught by the Ring ; and I say that because, when all is said and done, Vienna today, the living Vienna, is little but the Ring—plus, dimly, all that background of gothic and baroque which we have looked at all too superficially.

It has been said in these pages, I think with some emphasis, that Vienna is baroque, yet the Ring is certainly not baroque and is as certainly Vienna. But when we remember further assertions, made at various points of our itinerary, namely, that Vienna was (*a*) the Minoritenkirche, (*b*) the Stefansdom in the snow, (*c*) the 19th-century coffee-houses, (*d*) the Hofburg, (*e*) Schönbrunn, and so on, we are driven to the conclusion that our moods have misled us from time to time and that Vienna is all these things and more besides, notably the Ring. Nor will this really surprise us when we also recall that ancient if disputable saying that the whole is greater than the part.

Lost in contemplation of the glories of high baroque we alluded slightingly to the Ring ; that was a second impression. Our first impression, it may be remembered, was of a shining circlet of semi-precious stones, to repeat a hackneyed phrase ; and the first impression was, as first impressions have a way of being, a good deal nearer the truth than the second one. It all depends on the point of view. Arriving for the first time in Vienna we saw the Ring and its mighty buildings ; we remembered Covent Garden, Piccadilly Circus, Drury Lane, and Sadler's Wells—to say nothing of South Kensington and Trafalgar Square ; we remembered all that and we gasped ; it was as though all those places and institutions, with Buckingham Palace, the L.C.C., and London University thrown in, were wrought into one magnificent triumphal way, open to the sun and the breezes from high hills, em-bowered in sweet-scented limes.

But then, dreaming in the gardens of the Bel-vedere, lost in wonder at the creative impulse at its zenith, in a mood to brush aside impatiently any-thing that fell short of that perfection and sublime *conviction*, the thought of Semper's essays in a dis-carded form gave us a chilly shudder. By now, however, we have glimpsed enough of our city's history since the building of the Belvedere to make us see these innocent contributions in a warmer, mellower light and with slightly chastened eyes. We may, indeed, considering everything, consider-ing the speed and unerring purpose of the avalanche, be permitted to feel some wonder that this street

is as beautiful as it is. There was a good deal of rebuilding going on all over Europe during the last
half of the 19th century, some of it gallant, most of
it mean ; but nowhere else on all the Continent or
in England was there such a mighty show of determination to ignore decline and glorify the times
as we see embodied in this street.

A tour of it shall be our last promenade together.
No more suitable locality for a final harangue could
possibly be found : the street, as we have said, is
a closed circle which contains a city which no longer
grows, either physically or spiritually ; it is also, as
again we have said, much earlier, the formal admission of a decadence ; it is also, more practically, the
focus of that city's cultural life.

Some of the ingredients of that life we have
already glimpsed, since these are older than the
Ring. We know something, for instance, of the part
that the Hofburg has played in the development of
our city, and, considering the Habsburgs as patrons
of the arts, we took, for convenience, a long swoop
forward through time to see the assembled fruits
of their patronage which only in the 19th century
came to be housed in the immense museum opposite
the Hofburg. But the life of the theatre, which plays
so great a part in the lives of contemporary Viennese,
we have not glimpsed at all ; and the headquarters
of this too are on the Ring.

Let us agree that we are resting in the Burggarten ; no more charming place for that purpose
could be found. In the time of the Habsburgs it was
one of the very few palace gardens kept private

from the general public. Its smallness and unpre-
tentiousness reflects kindly upon its one-time owners
and emphasises the curious generousness which,
whether due to calculated policy or spontaneous
kindness, marked the later Habsburgs *vis-à-vis* their
property. Joseph started the tradition, I suppose as
a matter of principle, throwing open the Prater,
which was a deer-park, the Augarten in the Leopold-
stadt between the Danube and the Danube canal,
and other delightful resorts; but most of Joseph's
actions were cancelled, either by himself on his
deathbed or by his immediate successors, and it says
something for these that they made no attempt to
fence their lands. The Burggarten today is a tiny
oasis, beautifully timbered, at the heart of the city's
busiest, most fashionable quarter, and it still has
about it that peculiar air which for long envelopes
all things once private which have suddenly, by
force, been opened to the mob. It stands in the
shadow of the new wing of the Hofburg, and contains a fine gravelled terrace backed by conserva-
tories, now used as an open-air café, and, at a lower
level, leafy gardens for the lunch-hour refreshment
of tired office-workers. At night, in summer, there
is often an open-air concert of the kind in which
Vienna specialises, or even a small opera ; then,
sitting in the twilight, trying to forget the midges
and lose oneself in Mozart's exquisite invention (for
only the more careless Mozart is played here), one
is all the while acutely conscious of a huge dark
eagle with spread wings surmounting the wall of
the Burg, silhouetted against the paling sky.

Here, at any rate, we are sitting; peacefully, yet within a stone's throw of petrol-tainted streets. We have only to rise and follow a pleasant winding path to find ourselves out on the Ringstrasse itself. We have already observed the effect of this triple avenue of limes at its finest part, and here, turning to the right as we emerge, we are in the thick of it. This is the Burgring, called after the Hofburg, for the Ring is divided into many sections each with its own name. Since the war, however, with the absence of the steadying influence of the ruling house, the names have continually changed, and we must not be surprised if here and there we are already out of date.

The Burgring, I believe I am right in saying, has not changed, and it seems unlikely that it will. On the left it is completely taken up by the twin museums of art and natural history, on the right the immense and rambling buildings of the Burg itself, giving on to the gardens and the parade-ground called the Heldenplatz, these last approached from the Ring by an impressive and ponderous stone gateway. The museums, though spiritually gim-crack, make a splendid group in the Italian Renaissance style, and the whole composition—the two dark, ornate buildings with their cupolas, perfectly matched, facing each other across the ornamental gardens which form a setting for Maria Theresa and her generals; behind them, seen across the gardens, the low, cool stucco walls of the old Imperial stables —is pleasing and impressive in all but purist moods. For we too, it should be recalled, have in our veins the blood of the 19th century and we cannot deny this heritage, not entirely; if we did so we should also deny ourselves, turning to pale simulacra. Indeed, to stride along this boulevard on a fine morning in early spring with the snows unmelted on the encircling hills and the tender leaves of the lilacs still furled in their hardy casings, is, so dry and sparkling is the air, so immediate the quivering of natural life, to be exhilarated to the point of intoxication when all not only seems but actually *is* for the best in the best of possible worlds, and this great and smiling avenue is the high road to fulfilment, the promise of an abundant future, no longer the pompous cenotaph of a less abounding past. In that mood, which is a mood like any other and at least as valid as any other, standing in that great square composed of the twin museums and the Imperial stables on three sides and on the fourth the vast flat space in front of the Burg, broken by flower-beds and green lawns and flanked by the palace *Trakts*, glimpsing as one looks ahead the white marble of the Parliament buildings, catching the Rathaus spire above the tree-tops as they round the bend—in such a mood one experiences, one cannot escape experiencing unless by a conscious and perverted effort of will, something of the fine and sweeping enthusiasm of those 19th-century heralds who built thus in honour of a dawn which turned out to be a sunset.

There is too much talk of the *Föhn* in Vienna. It exists, true enough, and it doubtless adds to the natural dilatoriness of the Viennese, which is due

in the main to other causes; it can also infect the
stranger; but the *Föhn* does not blow every day.
In winter, when the whole city lies canopied in snow
and the trees on the Ring, now black and bony
fingered, are streaked as to stem and cushioned as
to bough with icy-cold, soft-crystalled white, and
the great east winds come sweeping in from the
plains, one frequently wishes it did. It is absent
too from these days of early spring when the sun
is shining through a crystal atmosphere of infinite
transparency and the perfect absence of humidity
makes the very act of breathing a subtle self-indulg-
ence. Then there is a quality about our city which
fills one again with hope for cities—not enormous
wens, but cities—and it is on the Ring that one finds
this quality most unobscured, for that street is wide
enough and open enough and verged enough with
natural soil, affording vistas, too, of natural hills, to
bring one close to the sky ; and at the same time,
in the midst of this healthy delight, we are also at
the heart of the highest manifestation of a city
culture with its arts, sciences, and politics ranged
side by side.

Coming at length to the sharpish bend which
marks the end of the Burgring and the Hofburg
grounds we find on the right the park-land still
continuing in the Volksgarten, on the left the
political shrines. It is a political part of the Ring,
but not unmitigatedly so, for half-way up, at the
end of the Volksgarten, stands the Burgtheater, and
farther on on the left the University ; here, in fact,
the arts, the sciences and politics rub shoulders. For

all that, the major emphasis is politics, municipal
and national. One cannot get away from them,
either in the name of the street or its memories.
Actually this stretch, running from the Palace of
Justice to the University, seems now to be divided
into two, called after famous men : the Dr. Ignaz
Seipel Ring, containing the Houses of Parliament,
and, farther on, the Dr. Karl Lueger Ring, containing the City Hall. But with no disrespect whatever
to these men of outstanding gifts, the first of whom,
in the days of the inflation, saved Austria from total
ruin by persuading a distrustful and apathetic
League of Nations into granting it a loan, and
the second of whom, as the first Christian Socialist
Burgomaster of Vienna, saved that city in the 19th
century from the disgrace of being ruled by financiers
and inflated tradesmen—with no disrespect to these,
it is impossible, unless one was born only yesterday,
to think of this section of the Ring as two. Originally
it was the Franzenring, after the emperor of that
name, and those who knew Imperial Vienna can
think of it as nothing else ; the present writer, who
did not, is obliged to think of it under the amazing
title of Der Ring des Zwölften Novembers, the 12th
of November, 1918, being the date of the revolution
and the official New Dawn. That was changed only
very recently after the gallant, harassed, misguided
and finally martyred Dr. Dollfuss had foolishly and
by fire suppressed the men who had made the 12th
of November a red-letter day. One is very much
afraid that before long there will be another
christening, and whatever events may lead up to

that will undoubtedly take place here, on this, the
most beautiful stretch of all the Ring, which already
has seen so much in the way of riot and bloodshed.
It is the natural forum of revolution. Here in
the precarious days of Socialist rule the peasants
and the workers clashed, burning down the Palace
of Justice ; here demonstrations are held at every
opportunity. One is glad, however, that when
Hitler murdered Dollfuss (by proxy, of course, re-
verting, very properly, to the technique of older
days), the Ring was not sullied by so evil-motived a
brawl. With a fine sense of fitness the old foreign
office in the Ballhausplatz was chosen for that deed,
this spot being closely linked with Prussian foolishness ; for there, on the direst plot of ground in
modern Europe, we have the centre of that system
of forged, suppressed, or precipitant telegrams which
the politicians found it necessary to establish before
the old, old Emperor could be prevailed upon to
consent to their demands, their too clever by half
demands, and the half-baked, half-hearted braggings
of the parvenu at Potsdam. Happily the Ballhausplatz is well away from the Ring, sheltered by the
Minoritenplatz and the Reichskanzleitrakt of the
Burg. One cannot traverse it without a chill. Doubtless there would sooner or later have been a war ;
but by all the portents the nucleus of that conflagration should have been the Wilhelmstrasse in
Berlin, a place fit for little else but the thinking up
of wars. Chance, however, gave that honour to
Vienna, as a reward for *Schlamperei* and the particular criminal negligence it showed in its choice

of foreign ministers. There is doubtless a curse on
that spot, though perhaps the ugly death there of
a brave chancellor has done something to remove
it. Happily it is hidden away. All foreign offices
should be hidden away, of course ; but as a rule they
are not. The bland façade, for instance, of No. 3,
Whitehall, is an outrage to all decent feeling ;
foreign offices are necessary, and so are sewers, and
with proper tact, or by an accident of genius, the
Viennese have placed theirs round a corner.

We have wandered away from the Ring and into
a darker world, for although the Ring has seen
atrocity and bloodshed it has been of a nobler kind,
the impotent fury of simple, harassed natures, of
peasants and working-men, doing their best to get
the world straight for peasants and working-men
and getting desperate with each other when they
find that under the present system their two aims
are at cross-purposes. On the Ring itself there is only
one reminder of Armageddon. That is on the far
side of the circle, on the Stubenring, which once
took the inflow of carriages from the city's most
palatial quarter in the neighbourhood of the Belvedere as they started out to take their places in
that brilliant corso on the Prater Hauptallee. It is
chiefly remarkable now for the huge building of the
war office, which calls itself No. 1, but which, with
its grey façade adorned with colossal representations
in stone of ancient helmets having the air of vast
grinning skulls, seems to take up most of one side.
If one is English it is impossible to pass this great
building without emotion. Those grey walls with

their arrogant emblems form the surviving shell of a brain, a controlling nerve-centre, which we fought for four years to destroy, and did. The emotion is weaker now than it was in the days when Austria had no more army to speak of ; we all have our armies now, built up to destroy or be destroyed. But even so, that building once ruled the destinies of an Imperial host, and, whether or not the Habsburgs are ever restored, the letters k.u.k. will never again be an emblem of mightiness. There is an irony about that building too, for it was one of the last of the great buildings of the Ring, that monument to Habsburg vainglory. It was not finished until 1913. . . .

But, heaven knows, we don't want to waste our time on current politics, finishing up with a dirty taste in our mouths ; we don't even want to be rude to Prussia, much less to Germany, in any irrevocable way. That country, on and off, for quite a number of decades has been giving the world a somewhat sickening display of what a country can do when it grants ascendancy to its brutal elements; but it may yet become, if it does not first annihilate the rest of Europe by forcing it into some lunatic suicide pact, a pattern to us all—in some respects, that is.

So we shall not even glance at the Parliament buildings and the Rathaus which stands back from its charming park, unless to say that in the latter, in the midst of all that 19th-century gothic (done a great deal better, it must be granted, than the gothic of that century was usually done), you can find the historical museum of the city of Vienna, which gives one better than anything else the detailed background of this city, bringing the whole thing alive. We shall even leave the University alone, for all cities have such things; nor shall we go any farther in the direction we have taken, for, past the University, past the Votive Church of St. Saviours with its twin open-work spires to the memory of Franz Josef's escape from assassination at the hands of the Hungarian tailor, Libényi, we should stumble upon the Bourse, which would be unfortunate, that being the grisly spider of the days of the inflation. We are not concerned now with the similarities between Vienna and other great capitals of Europe, but with the differences. Symbolic of these differences is the great Burgtheater, opposite the Rathaus, and the even greater Opera House which we left immediately behind us, at the foot of the Kärntnerstrasse, when we began to wander round the Ring. We shall not go all the way round after all.

We have talked a good deal of the softness of the Viennese, of their lack of intellectual vigour, and of the historical causes of this. As one would expect, Vienna has produced few great writers, none at all in the highest flight, for great writers, even when their thinking is confused, do not flourish in an atmosphere of intellectual timidity caused by a rigid and perennial censorship. This, indeed, is commonly offered as the only reason for Vienna's inferiority in letters and her supremacy in music; but it is not so simple as that. The social conditions prevailing throughout the last three hundred years have undoubtedly been far more propitious for the composer than for the writer, since the work of the former does not visibly reflect his political opinions; in his private thoughts he may be as subversive as he likes, but it will be hard to prove, even to the satisfaction of a secret police, that any given symphony is in fact a revolutionary document. In the world of beauty unrelated by any standard images to the problems of society the artist may move uncurbed, and in this exclusive world the composer is most at home. But the association of Vienna pre-eminently with music, though encouraged by these considerations, must have deeper causes, and, far from attempting to analyse these here, I shall not even venture to suggest that such an analysis is anywhere possible, although it may be. To discover and balance all the contributory elements of a national temperament would take more than a single lifetime. But if the creative impulse of a nation were, so to speak, a substance in suspension, waiting for the shape of the times to precipitate it into the most suitable form, we should surely find in Vienna not only music in a state of high development, but painting also ; for the painter, too, has access to that realm of abstract beauty, even though he must take with him into it more of the paraphernalia of everyday life than the musician, who need take none at all. But we do not find this. Vienna, like any other city, has produced her painters, the Grans and Rottmayrs of the baroque, the Makarts, the Canons, the Schindlers of the 19th century ; yet although they deserve more notice than they receive outside Vienna they are minor talents indeed. In fact, the only artists whose voices are heard with any clarity against the sweet clamour of the great musicians are the architects of the turn of the 17th century.

But, whatever the causes, music is in the air, and by music I do not necessarily mean music of a high philosophical content, but music as a lyrical expression. Austria, more than any country apart from Italy, is the home of that ; the waltz alone is sufficient proof. It is partly due to the censorship of ideas, no doubt ; it may also be partly due to the fact that music, among many other things, is the natural voice of nostalgia, and oppressed peoples take refuge in the indulgence of nostalgia which they express in song, and the Austrian provinces, from Tyrol to Transylvania, have always, by English standards, been oppressed. Also there is something in the Viennese which makes them still prefer to find their stimulus in public displays rather than in private meditation, for hand in hand with their love of music goes a passion for the theatre.

That brings us back to the celebrated Burgtheater before which we have been standing all this time. It was round this building, together with the Opera, that the cultural life of 19th-century Imperial Vienna so showily revolved. This theatre at its apogee must have been, with the Comédie Française, the finest in the world, starred with the names of three such great actors as Sonnenthal, Levinski and the legendary Kainz. Josef Kainz was born with none of the graces of an actor ; his natural voice was poor, but he trained it until it was an instrument of unsurpassed virtuosity ; he was short, yet he could have played a giant ; he was not handsome. By sheer force of genius he overcame his disabilities. He died in 1910 at the early age of fifty-two, but records of his voice are in existence and through the mist of scratchiness those travestied tones loom forth with in them still enough of the man to supply some idea of the greatness of his total presence. There is no Kainz in Vienna now, but it is still a city of fine acting. The Burgtheater has behind it a magnificent tradition, not merely of favoured stars but of an old-established repertory company with every member an *expert* in his art. It is fashionable nowadays to laugh at the Burg-theater style as hollow and outworn, and indeed there are often passages of painful emptiness where the lines are recited in the traditional way with none of the inner conviction upon which the style arose. But one can still see there fine acting and hear con-vincing declamation of a kind which, alas, is dead in England, bolder and larger than life. And it should not be forgotten that all through that period when England had fine acting and prostituted it to non-sense like *The Bells*, in Vienna, a city in decline, a city made soft by ceaseless harassings, these great actors of the heyday of the Burgtheater drew crowded houses to the greatest dramas in existence, as their smaller successors still do.

Indeed, of all things in Vienna acting is in the liveliest case. The art of the theatre seems to be the one thing that has not stopped developing. For those who cannot stand Shakespeare being acted in the grand manner there is, in a near-by theatre, the Theater in der Josefstadt, a commercial stage, more-over, not a state-aided one, a school of naturalistic acting which emphasises still more the barrenness of our London theatre. At the Burgtheater the play is a great and often deeply moving spectacle, aiming at and sometimes touching grandeur; by the word " spectacle " I do not mean a show of lavishness, but simply that the audience is apart from the hap-penings on the stage and consciously looking on. At the Theater in der Josefstadt, on the other hand, the audience is immersed and lost in the movement of the stage. The mood is established and the whole theatre becomes a part of it. This is true naturalism, the naturalism, allowing for differences in national temperament, of Stanislavski and the Moscow Art Theatre. It also is seen to be slightly larger than life, as all art must be. Beside this our West-end stage has an air of simpering, self-conscious, hackneyed make-believe ; no longer bold enough to swagger, lacking the humility to surrender to the play-wright's mood, it raises its silly head and bleats, filled with smug complacency at the softness of its tones.

But although the spoken drama, and particularly on these two stages, is a pivotal point of Viennese life, even more so is the opera, which, at the same time, is less alive. This tremendous institution has been directed by many great men from Gluck to Mahler, and although it is dying for lack of new

material it remains a shrine. The present great
building in Ringstrasse French-Renaissance style
is new, of course, but the tradition can be traced
back through several theatres, including the oldest
of all Vienna's stages, the Theater an der Wien.
(This, some little way outside the Inner City, was
built at the end of the 18th century for Schikaneder,
the producer, and the concocter of the recondite
libretto of Mozart's *Magic Flute*.)

It is to all appearances a cosmopolitan opera house
of the most rampageous sort. But it is better than
that. It, too, has a first-class repertory company, and
although in the last days of Imperial Vienna it must
have been a hot-bed of fashion it also served music.
At the back of the stalls, beneath the spacious diplomatic box, there is a standing-place which gives a
small and close-packed mass of people a perfect view
of the stage for a shilling or two a head ; and, before
the deluge, part of this space was roped off and kept
as a free standing-place for k.u.k. officers in uniform.
If that does not show that beneath all the glitter
that audience had a genuine love of music nothing
can. Who can imagine a squad of subalterns of
His Britannic Majesty's Army attending an opera
at all, much less standing throughout the performance ?

And yet with all this love of music, music is also
dying in Vienna. For as long as it has been cultivated
as an independent and self-conscious art Vienna has
been the headquarters of music, attracting not only
the musicians of Austria, but also foreigners like
Beethoven and Brahms. But the process has ceased ;

even the harassed native composers have to go elsewhere for recognition. Vienna is bound by the Ring, the closed circle, it wants nothing new, and no more convincing demonstration of her weariness can be found than this stagnation of her most vital part. Music was already dying fast in the days of Mahler, who strove as conductor of the Philharmonic Orchestra to eliminate the dead forms of a lesser decadence while as a composer he burnt himself out in his feverish efforts to push the greater decadence to far and beautiful limits in a bold and passionately nervous exploration of his individuality. As a composer, that is, he was an artist of the decadence of Europe, which was established when Mozart died, a prophet of a hieratic order; while as a conductor he strove to stop the rot, the stereotyped approach which was killing the glories of the decadence itself. But Mahler is many years dead, and since him nothing has happened in Vienna that is also *of* Vienna. His own compositions, above all his *Kindertötenlieder* and *Das Lied von der Erde*, we value as exquisite and exotic flowers, as the Blue Flowers, one might almost say, of the decadence. They mark the end of the process which started in Mozart, without his knowledge, becoming ever more self-conscious as ever more acutely it felt its detachment from the popular drift. And, fitly enough, Mahler is the last composer of true greatness recognised by Vienna as a city. The tone of Vienna's musical life is set by the Philharmonic Orchestra, which Mahler reformed and which now, apart from Richard Strauss and a few

smaller men, plays no music at its celebrated concerts that Mahler did not know. It is static.

The deep past we have been able to view in solid
blocks, as it were, regarding it with detachment as
one regards the exhibits of a museum, pinned down
under glass. But from the time of Mozart past and
present have been so inextricably intertangled that
nowhere can be found a vantage point so unambiguously of the present day that one can stand upon it
with a banner emblazoned with a confident motto
bidding farewell to the past. . . . Unless, of course,
on the roof of the Karl Marx Hof, or the Amalienbad,
those genuine masterpieces of the post-war Socialist
municipality. Ten years ago, indeed, these might
have suggested themselves for such a purpose,
but since then the one has been shattered by the
shells of an advancing barbarism, while, as for
the other—it takes more than a municipal bath-
ing establishment to wash away the accumulated
years.

One cannot regard with detachment the exhibits
of a museum of which one forms a part; and Vienna
today is itself very like a museum, the distant past
merely forming a crowded gallery within the whole;
and of that containing edifice everybody in Vienna,
everybody who finds the life of the place to his liking
and himself cares to follow it if only for a time,
becomes a part. If he does not he goes mad. *Wiener
Leben*, the theme of pleasant waltzes, the delicious
legend, is also a fact; reality being less selective
than art, the real version has its drawbacks, but also

The Belvedere

Tombs of the Emperors

its enchantments. As pursued in this lovely city on
the fringe of 20th-century Europe life takes on,
when seen from afar, very much the air of something under glass; but there come short moments
when even now it seems to carry sufficient vitality
to make it the unique, still palpitating nucleus of
a corpse-like realm. We are talking, naturally, of
the Europe of great cities; many countrysides are
still alive, and the most vital of them all, outside
the Latin lands, is Austria herself, that scratch
collection of hereditary duchies and archduchies left
by the inspired map-readers of Versailles to feed a
crippled metropolis—as well as itself. . . . We shall,
before taking leave of Vienna, have to consider that
countryside if only for a moment, turning for encouragement from the dying to the living. Were
Vienna dynamic instead of static, if it were possible
to believe in some miraculous recovery, the country
and its capital would be a model to the world. As
it is we can learn from it.

Compare our English situation. Here we have
neither one thing nor another, neither the glorious
relic of a fading city-culture nor the roots of a thriv-
ing rural culture. Until the early 19th century
London stood for a city culture of a kind (as Vienna
did until the deluge, as she still, faintly but clearly,
does). That was destroyed by a national predilection
for tradesmen and money-lenders, by, in short, the
rise of a middle class which neither worked with
its hands nor had any time for the graces of life.
Until that time, too, and indeed for some little time
after, England also had a rural culture of a kind.

That went in the same way. London, as a community, now has the soul of a sixpenny store; and it, with other emulative wens, has blighted all the countryside. It is when one looks at this side of the picture that Vienna still seems to hold the vital spark; but looked at from the other side she is seen to have laid herself down to die—to die peacefully and naturally of slow and inevitable exhaustion, as a fatalist may die, his features composed, the ghost of a smile on his lips, so that even in death when it comes at last there is the illusion that life still sleeps beneath that waxen mask. . . . While London, twisted, gnarled in the furious struggle to preserve herself, or rather not herself but *life*, devoured by hideous cancers, still lives somehow, toughly hanging on. And since the doctrine of the sacredness of life is supreme in Western Europe, though in Vienna weakened, perhaps, by Asiatic airs, we must struggle to preserve it. But life, *qua* life, is a primitive process, and even as we struggle on, like some ancient termagant smitten by stroke after stroke, we may, in the intervals of fighting for our breath, envy those who can let it go more gracefully and easily—but not for long.

Also we have something that Vienna has not got. We have the freedom of the mind. We may not keep it much longer; all over Europe bigotry and superstition rears its cobra head; but for centuries we have had a sort of freedom, and those who know how can use it still. It has led us into dreadful places, into, for instance, the black evil of sentimental materialism. And even from this we may be emerg-

ing only into a larger lunacy. But although it is best
to be free and clear-headed it is better to be free and
blundering than to have the clearest sight in the
world and be in chains. Out of our appalling welter
of blackness and smoke something may yet come,
if not for our own land directly, perhaps first for
another with a younger mind ; for men of great
gifts and brains have been able to go their ways,
attached at first to material ends, then later and
more alone penetrating still more boldly, unsup-
ported but unchecked, if only because the mass is
sunk too deep in apathy to pay close attention to
their voyagings and want to stop them. There is a
curious parallel there. . . . In Vienna, on the other
hand, the brain has either been killed or turned in
on itself; music has been its expression, and music-
ally it is dying if not dead as far as creation is concerned, and creation is life: yet our freedom, and
the good and bad uses we have made of it, including
the sowing of seed for an unknown future in some
unpredictable quarter of the globe, we owe very
much to that city out of which nothing more new
is likely to come—not at any rate until Europe has
been turned upside down once more, and, as we
know it, no longer exists.

All that, of course, is a manner of saying. The
actual daily life of the Viennese continues still and
is frequently enjoyed. The young live in hopes—
even then, though they may work and die for their
clashing political ideals, not what we should call
hopes. There is still eating and drinking and the
joy of living, still the apprehension of beauty. There

is incessant music of the finest order—but the last composer played by the Philharmonic Orchestra is Richard Strauss. There is a good deal of writing— but the last writer of genius occurring in Vienna was Anton Schnitzler. Science and medicine are still exalted—but the last great Viennese doctor was Sigmund Freud. . . .

Strauss—Schnitzler—Freud. . . . You cannot, it seems to me, build much on that. But at least these manifestations are the logical outcome of a Mozart followed by a Schubert followed by a Hugo Wolf. *That* picture, if nothing else, is finished. It might have been our picture, too, in essence, if we hadn't all suddenly taken to digging for coal—and even coal does not last for ever.

By that picture our culture must stand or fall, for coal, although it has spoilt the last hundred years for us, doubtless has in it the germ of a future age which will know what to do with the stuff. Of course, it both stands *and* falls.

Farther than that one really cannot go without stepping boldly on to ground that simply does not exist. There is amusement and possibly instruction to be had in looking back and tracing processes and being wise after the event; it is not unhelpful for the present. But the final foolishness is to indulge in any prophecy which takes one far ahead. All that Vienna shows us is really the smallest and most insignificant of cycles, the rise and fall of a culture which has lasted the length of a single dynasty, a small part only of the history we know and the merest fragment of all that is yet to come.

There are, no doubt, many who would deny the validity of this dying culture, which we have seen mirrored in the buildings of a city, the culture which had a flowering in baroque Vienna, because the full enjoyment of it was limited to so few, and those unworthy. Many too will hear nothing good of it because of the destinies accorded its two most gifted men, Mozart and Schubert. Others may point to the peasants of the countryside with their songs and painted houses and ask what these city cultures are all about. There seems to me a false perspective here, an unwarranted stress on the what might have been and an ignoring of what not only is but also must be. The argument would run that there is no good in this so-called culture because it has failed so utterly and abjectly to live up to its highest potentialities. That is a doctrinaire approach. What are its highest potentialities, in any case? The only way to look at Schubert's death and still keep sane is with unfading astonishment and gratitude that this man was born at all, and, being born, somehow kept alive for nearly thirty years, a tiny sparkle of infinite brilliance glittering in the semi-darkness.

As for the peasants, the uncountable masses who have never heard of Schubert and who form the vast majority (not only in Europe, the merest maritime fringe of a single great geographical continent, but in all the rest of that continent and in others as well), their lives have a certain richness, some of them, and one day they will be richer still, if all continues as it has gone until now. The notion of progress is not a popular one just now with the

majority; we most of us laugh at that; but what
we are laughing at, really, is not the idea of progress
as such, but the 19th-century notion that the
world leaps visibly forward every decade. There is,
quite obviously, some kind of progress persisting,
but infinitely slow and with one and a half steps
backward for every two forward. As culture follows
culture to the casual eye it looks very much as
though what is gained on the roundabouts is lost
on the swings; it is, nearly, but not quite. There
seems to be always an infinitesimal gain. Pythagoras
knew more than the mathematicians of the Renaissance, but we know more than Pythagoras. And
there is a difference between the peasants of today
and the men of the stone age. These passing cultures
seem, in fact, to be for their especial benefit. The
rise of civilisation, by which I mean the rudimentary
universal civilisation, is so fabulously slow that it is
difficult to find an image for it. One is forced into
comparing it with the formation of the crust of the
earth, which is even a little slower. The dry land
slowly emerges from the sea, taking millennia to do
it. It is not invariably level. The internal forces,
operating with greater force in certain places, throw
up now here, now there, mighty mountain ranges,
and these ranges are our various intensive cultures.
The difference between the low land and the heights
is at first immense, but slowly, through more
millennia, billennia, one should say, it diminishes.
Erosion does its work and the heights are reduced
and the lowlands slightly raised. That is neither a
perfect analogy nor an accurate statement of

scientific fact, but science can look after itself, and as for analogies, these are not sought as self-contained objects of art, perfect in all their parts; they are the tentative flights of groping minds and nothing more.

We have come too far from Vienna and its Ring. We started out not to make futile and impertinent guesses at the riddle of the Sphinx but to gaze with sympathetic eyes on a scene which forms our immediate heritage and on which we must soon turn our backs. We desired to catch a mood that is dying, realising that whatever may come, dark age or fresh renaissance, judicial contemplation of the past may steady us a little. We chose Vienna because it shows us a completed picture, peculiarly uncomplicated, and because the past is so much in its present.

It was said some pages back that nothing seems anachronistic in Vienna for the simple reason that there is nothing but anachronism there. You find this quality fixed in an opera by Richard Strauss, that opera which was also mentioned as a mirror of the Viennese culture untranscendentalised: the *Rosenkavalier*. There an 18th-century sort of plot is narrated by an artist of the decadence, contemporary with Schnitzler, and played out against a rococo background; the illustrative music is orchestrated with an early 20th-century luxuriance and is based on the rhythm of the 19th-century waltz. The whole work is compact of anachronism, yet it is perfectly right. The libretto, in style, should have been of an arid classicism. The music should have been orchestrated in the manner of Salieri and based on the gavotte. But Vienna is not like that, and Strauss and von Hofmannsthal between them have perfectly captured Vienna as it is, or very recently was, a kind of shining, slightly vulgar synthesis of all these modes, from Schönbrunn to the modern parts of the Hofburg on the Ring. Submitting to those exotic and often exquisite strains which so perfectly seem to reflect the spirit of Imperial Vienna in its final phase, the fine physical exuberance touched with delicate sentimentality, the sentimental bubble pricked by the laughter of a cheerful cynicism, one feels for the moment that this is all, that this is the whole of Vienna, a charming fantasy with no roots in any reality at all.

But we are wrong; the roots are there. Outside the theatre, on the brilliantly lighted Ring, the interiors of expensive cafés shining through the artificial trees, you may take a tram—it is still only ten o'clock, for the theatres start early in Vienna ; and this tram in something over half an hour, clattering through the suburbs of the city, will bring you to Vienna's limits at the foot of the wooded hills, to an outer suburb which has still a nucleus of village life. We have chosen an evening in autumn for our purpose, and here, so close to our proud and shining monument of a culture in decline, of which we have talked so much, there is nothing but the stillness of the countryside containing the sounds of village life, dim gossiping groups in the shadow of whitewashed cottage walls, a hand accordion wheezing out the tune of a waltz or something much older than that, a burst of sturdy laughter through the open windows of an inn. And the heavy evening air, slightly misted with vapours from the Danube far below, is loaded further with the smell of autumn leaves and the turned soil of the vineyards.

We have come here because of the vineyards. They have been here through immemorial times; many have been built over, but no matter how far out Vienna pushes there will always be vineyards close by to produce the sourish, sweetish local wines to be drunk in every café and *Lokal* throughout the city. We are seeking a house with a " bush ", which proclaims that some small cultivator has gathered his grapes and pressed them and made his wine which is not to be bottled and sold away but drunk then and there, on the spot, unfermented. The bush is a bundle of pine-boughs which will hang there until the wine runs out. The wine is called Heuriger wine.

There is no need to describe the scene in the inn or the garden where this age-long ritual is being performed. Long ago we visited the Prater and shared in the evening relaxation of the people there. Here it is very much like that, but on a far smaller, more intimate scale, with a good deal of singing and a certain heightened consciousness of well-being. There are fashionable Heurigers, but this is a meeting of the people for the people, and here among the cheerful poor, the manual labourers, the smallest officials, the men who work in the skirting fields and vineyards, we realise the fallacy of every generalisation as to " softness ", or " hardness ", or " intellectual tenacity ". These are simply the people, the sturdy stock to which every culture must be grafted and which survives the decay of the bloom. Vienna has its roots.

. . . Or again, back once more in the heart of the city, we walk on a Christmas Eve up the narrow, neon-lighted canyon of the Kärntnerstrasse, dazzled by the glittering displays of the bright and bandbox-like shop windows. And suddenly we reach the end and step into comparative darkness, and look up at the roof of the cathedral, perhaps with snow on it, and the dim spire pointing to the stars. And from somewhere high up in that tower, from that plat-form, no doubt, whence we had our great view of the arena of Habsburg Europe, the Marchfeld, there comes down to us the lonely sound of trumpets, scarcely interrupted by the desultory midnight traffic, playing in solemn unison some infinitely slow and simple round—a handful of trumpeters high up above the ancient city sounding their homage on the anniversary of Christendom in the cold and hollow spaces of the mediaeval tower, their accents floating out on the dark, crisp air beneath the stars. . . .

The Belvedere is dead, but the Stefansdom still lives, a piece of the days when men were blind and superstitious but still working and building with their brains and with their hands. The spirit persists, slightly more enlightened, untended, unencouraged in an infinite multitude of half-starved souls, and one day, when the dead stuff of the blooming time is cleared away, it will creep up again like young grass to make a field for another summer flowering.

THE END

Printed in Great Britain by R. & R. CLARK, LIMITED, *Edinburgh.*

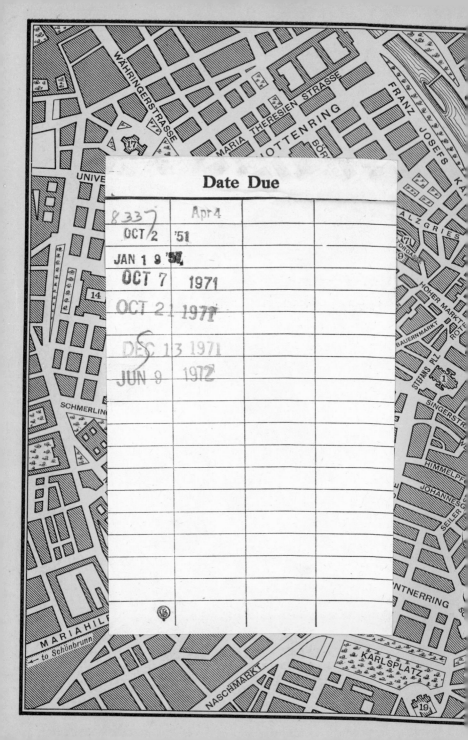

Date Due

8 337	Apr 4		
OCT 2 '51			
JAN 1 9 '52			
OCT 7 1971			
OCT 21 1971			
DEC 13 1971			
JUN 9 1972			